PRAISE FOR *A Dream Too Big*

"I loved this story of triumph in praise of a sacrificial single mom and a kid who, against all odds, fought hunger pains and gangs to make dreams-too-big become a dream-come-true. Through gunshots and temptations of inner-city poverty, Caylin Moore laced up his cleats, outran gangs, and caught the 6:00 a.m. bus on an empty stomach. A future world-changer, Caylin has penned an inspiring tale that should be mandatory reading for every student, parent, and anyone else interested in the success of those who will shape and define our future."

—Ron Hall, #1 *New York Times* bestselling author of *Same Kind of Different as Me* and *Workin' Our Way Home*

"*A Dream Too Big* is a truly special book. Caylin's story is not just inspirational, it is instructional. I have admired him and his journey for a long time; read this book and you'll understand why."

—Wes Moore, CEO of Robin Hood and bestselling author of *The Other Wes Moore*

A Dream Too Big

A Dream Too Big

The Story of an Improbable Journey from Compton to Oxford

Caylin Louis Moore

An Imprint of Thomas Nelson

Published in Nashville, Tennessee, by Nelson Books, an imprint of Thomas Nelson. Nelson Books and Thomas Nelson are registered trademarks of HarperCollins Christian Publishing, Inc.

ISBN 978-1-4002-0992-7 (eBook)
ISBN 978-1-4002-0991-0 (HC)

Library of Congress Control Number: 2018964312

Printed in the United States of America

19 20 21 22 23 LSC 10 9 8 7 6 5 4 3 2 1

To Mom.

To the spirit of my ancestors.

To the dead homies, rest in peace.

Contents

Introduction

I didn't start out with the goal of becoming a Rhodes Scholar. As a kid, I didn't even know what a Rhodes Scholar was. If I had known, I would have seen it as most people around me did: a dream too big for a kid from Compton. But that wouldn't have stopped me from dreaming it. I've always dreamed big. For some people, that's been a problem.

You see, in underserved inner-city communities like Compton, people don't always like dreamers. Gangs look at a dreamer and think, *He'll never be one of us. And if he isn't one of us, he's a problem.* Bad teachers look at a dreamer and think, *That boy needs to know his place.* Many people look at a dreamer and think, *He'll never succeed outside of shooting a basketball or rapping over a beat.* Sometimes even neighbors and family members think dreamers are up to no good, because who would dare to have big dreams in such a place?

They all think those things, but the truth goes deeper.

Dreamers who reach high and strive to rise illustrate the stark realities of those who are left feeling like it's better to just stay down than to climb and risk falling. Kids trapped in the same circumstances start off as dreamers too. Every kid I knew in elementary school had big dreams. But the dreams slowly faded away as the reality of dilapidated schools, gang violence, the unbalanced criminal justice system, and the lack of family support networks began to set in. Who can blame those kids when their environment has been molded by oppression, these systems ingrained long before their grandparents were even a thought? Living within the confines of what others tell you is possible is all they have ever known. A dreamer can also make outsiders think he is a threat to the status quo. It's hard for a dreamer to find his place in this world. Any dreams coming from an inner-city neighborhood are tentative and can easily die from malnourishment. They are all dreams too big as far as a lot of people are concerned.

I've never let that stop me.

My first big dream was to make it to the NFL. I dreamed of using the NFL to change the lives of the people in my community, in my world. I worked hard to reach that goal, but I didn't make it my only priority. Here's the surprising part: the pursuit of that goal led me to even greater dreams. Achievements in academics, pursued to expand my opportunities for a football career, earned me scholarships to two great colleges. And those environments opened my eyes to the potential of education, to the possibility of changing the world in a way I never could imagine doing as a professional football player. My college experiences then led me to apply for scholarships. I was awarded several, including a Fulbright and, ultimately, the Rhodes Scholarship.

Along the way, I cofounded the Texas Christian University student organization TCU SPARK (Strong Players Are Reaching Kids) and began to speak across the United States to any corporation, university, prison, or gang that would be willing to hear my voice. Those experiences helped me realize what I wanted to do with my life. I wanted to help. I wanted one day to know how it feels to have changed the world. I wanted to put big dreams within reach of young people as well as anybody who seeks to better themselves and the world we live in. This book is my story, and I want my story to inspire. Most of all, I want it to provide hope to people who might be having a hard time holding on to it.

I've been brutally hungry, so much so that it seemed like the pains in my stomach might never go away. I've been treated like a throwaway person, given no due by an inner-city educational system that is not only broken but punitive. I've known crushing poverty. I've had guns flashed at me as I walked home from school, and I've lost friends to senseless violence.

If all that has taught me anything, it's that you can get

by without food for a time. You can be cold and hungry. You can survive poverty, and you can transition from victim of violence to victor over violence. It is only when you give up hope that you will be beaten and lost. A wise man once told me a well-known saying: "Man can live about forty days without food, about three days without water, about eight minutes without air, but not for one moment without hope." In the words of Dr. Martin Luther King Jr.: "We must accept finite disappointment, but never lose infinite hope." The greatest hope lies in dreams that seem too big to be realized. Audacious dreams that you have no right even thinking about.

Competing for a Rhodes Scholarship was part of my still-ongoing journey, and the process was enlightening. During the final interview for the scholarship, the questions posed to candidates are intellectual, largely related to a given candidate's interests. In my interview, I was able to make the questions personal and relate them to my life experiences. The interview was an entrance into a new world. The Rhodes Scholarship, with a history rooted in colonial imperialism and consisting of individuals drawn from the world's elite, is about as far removed from where I come from as is possible to imagine. Nevertheless, the interviewers wanted to hear about my dreams, and their questions implied that they believed my dreams might help others. I already knew in my heart this was true, but it was clarifying to discover others might think so too.

Question by question, the interview gave me a chance to tell the Rhodes committee my story. It's what won me a scholarship and is why I've chosen specific questions from that interview to introduce each chapter in this book. The questions describe the journey and the themes that define me; each one represents a signpost I've followed on my quest to be my very best.

If there's a key message here, one thing I want readers to take away from reading this book, it's that you have to dream dreams that are too big. Dreams that are on the edge of impossibility to everyone else, but live on the edge of possibility in your heart. Dreams worth fighting for. You don't have to win every fight, but you have to fight every fight. It makes no sense to let the possibility and fear of failure get in the way of trying. Have dreams that scare you. Dreams so big that, when you close your eyes, the best your mind can bring forth into your consciousness pales in comparison to the magnificent reality of them. Many years ago, I committed myself to dreaming dreams that were so big, so unimaginable, so unfathomable, so unrealistic, that without divine intervention they were destined to fail. They were all dreams too big. And this book is the story of how they came true.

1

QUESTION: *"How do you get people on board to try to change these social issues?"*

Things could have been so much different. I could have lived the rest of my life like I did the first six, safe and secure in a place where all the dangers of the hood were far away, were something you only see on TV. I think one word sums up the first six years of my life, in the Inland Empire suburb of Fontana: *insulated*.

Fontana is an upper-middle-class, mostly white city about sixty miles east of Los Angeles, shoehorned between San Bernardino and Rancho Cucamonga. It is the polar opposite of Compton, where I grew up. Living in Fontana was like living in one of those TV commercials featuring a happy family in a bright, sunny, and tidy suburban house. You know, the State Farm commercial or the Procter & Gamble ad, with the token perfect black family all smiling around a brand-new kitchen table, sun pouring through squeaky-clean windows. My father was a barber and my mom worked in medical management while studying for her law degree at night. My mom likes to say that we were the Huxtables, the picture-perfect family on *The Cosby Show*. Only we had a dark side, hidden deep.

That darkness was my father. Although my mother

shielded us, and I wouldn't understand the extent of it for years, he psychologically, emotionally, and verbally abused my mother. As a father, he was at best distant. He was medium brown-skinned, tall, muscular, and extremely good-looking. Even though he had an ideal family and big house in a suburban paradise, he was a deeply unhappy man who harbored an unreasonable anger inside him.

What I wouldn't know until I was an adult was that my father was a victim of abuse by his stepfather when he was young, and he felt his mother failed to protect his emotional and physical well-being. As the reality set in, my father's innocence and childhood were lost, and he never received the help that he needed to recover from those wounds. I don't think my mom even knew about all that until much later. When he finally did tell her, he told my mom that he married her because he thought she could fix him.

I never saw my father laugh, and I rarely saw him smile. He was a control freak. It could have been a tendency that he developed in response to the control that was taken from him as a child. That didn't work too well when mixed with my mom's tendency of being unstructured and free-spirited at times. If you didn't do things exactly the way he wanted them done, there would be hell to pay. And, a lot of times, there was no telling how he wanted things done, or what he wanted done just wasn't reasonable. Like all control freaks, he was really trying to control everything about life. But life doesn't work that way. He once got mad that I had wet my bed as a three-year-old. His solution? Make me walk around in a black garbage bag fashioned as a diaper, after spanking me until I cried.

So it wasn't surprising that I grew up with a combination of respect and fear for the man. Even so, I can remember the rare light moments, like my dad dancing in the living room with my sister and me. I remember him teaching me to ride my bicycle, out in front of the house. I remember being five years old and holding his hand as we walked into the barbershop where he worked. I was so happy to shake the other barbers' hands. My father let me sit and watch the fish swimming around in the huge aquarium tank that stood in the middle of the shop.

He wasn't a man you expected a hug from, and I would have been shocked if he had ever consoled me over something like a scraped knee. I stayed out of his way, which wasn't all that hard because he had little to do with us kids. When it came to potty training, my mom even taught me how to stand when I pee. She would put cheerios into the toilet bowl and tell me to aim and sink them, as if they were battleships. Taking care of us—mentally, physically, emotionally—fell to my mom. We were *her* children. I thank God for that, because I was more influenced by, and grew up to be more like, my mom. My father's anger is not a weight I would wish on anyone, and I'm glad I don't carry that burden.

My mom made my childhood wonderful, because she understood me. After my first day of kindergarten, she picked me up from day care. She noticed I was upset and asked, "What's wrong, baby?"

"Miss Gallagher told me to do my homework when I got home."

"Okay, well come on, honey. We'll do your homework." But when she looked through my folder, she saw that I had done it all at day care.

"Well, this is really good—your homework is done, baby."

"No, she told me to do my homework *at home*. But I'm home, and I have no homework." Tears of frustration rolled down my chubby cheeks.

She got it. She knew that I was tenacious and wanted to get the most out of every opportunity in front of me. *Exactly* as it was supposed to be done. I wanted to go above and beyond the homework and the standard that was set for me and achieve more than was expected. That was true even as a kindergartner. So rather than just laugh and tell me I was being silly, my mom started making extra homework for me every day so I would have some to do at home. My mom saved up for three months to purchase the first computer she ever owned in her life. She'd create a list of spelling exercises or simple math problems and then print them out for me to do. Sometimes I would even take the homework she had created for me to school the next morning, turning it in with the homework I'd been assigned by the teacher.

I loved school from the start. Sugar Hill Elementary was a few cities over in Moreno Valley, where we moved when I was five. It reflected the same pride and values that homeowners in Fontana enjoyed. They considered themselves progressive and enlightened, and put money and time into their schools. I was never made to think about the color of my skin or how I was different from my classmates, even though I was one of only three black kids in my class. I was surrounded mostly by white people, but I never encountered racism. Certainly there were many things I couldn't know, things said in kitchens and living rooms down the street, real estate agents encouraging black families to purchase homes only in certain areas, or what someone might think to himself passing by my family in the grocery store. Nothing that I would be conscious of as a kid. The most important color in a place like Moreno Valley is green. Can you afford it? Because if you can, you're like everyone else there. You've paid your admission fee, and you're welcomed. The fact is, the first time I ever heard the N-word was after we moved to Compton.

Life in Fontana and Moreno Valley was calm, comfortable, and easy. At least for me. I spent so many pleasant hours just playing with my older sister Mi. Mi was an incredibly fun sibling, always looking for interesting things to do. I would happily sit on the floor in her room, playing beside her: Mi with her yellow suburban Barbie house and cool red truck, me with my log cabin complete with its own tool shed and a dunc buggy jeep. My younger brother Chase was little and pretty much played whatever Mi encouraged us to play. It was our version, however simple, of the American Dream.

School was part of that dream. Unlike later in Compton, the environment at Sugar Hill Elementary was kind, patient, and professional. Even loving. Robin Gallagher was my kindergarten teacher, a ginger-haired thirtysomething who was—in body type and personality—completely huggable. She was the consummate kindergarten teacher, equal parts kind mentor and patient, guiding instructor. She started and ended each school day with the same bright, beaming smile, as if she were so incredibly happy to see all her students.

My best friend in school was Michael, a poor white kid who lived in a trailer park. He had the most ragged clothes of anyone in the school, along with unkempt hair and a snaggletooth smile. But even he wasn't ostracized. And, in turn, he acted like everyone else. He was one of the nicest, most fun, and most respectful kids in our class. That was the Sugar Hill way. And, consequently, I never thought of him as being different—economically or culturally—until much later when I looked back at those rose-tinted years.

Moreno Valley wasn't a place where you dwelled on the bad. Traumas were kept contained and limited. In my first year at Sugar Hill, Andrea—one of the twin girls who were the other two black kids in my class—was playing out in front of her house. I imagine Andrea was chasing a ball or running away from her sister in a game of tag. She ran out between two parked cars into the street and was hit by a car, killed by someone just driving to Ralphs Grocery.

Everyone was saddened by her death. I was sad too. But because I was so insulated, so far removed from thinking the same thing might happen to me, I was mostly sad that I had lost someone to play with. School went on. I went on. As if by silent agreement, we all moved on as quickly as decorum allowed and put her death behind us. We just didn't talk about her anymore. It was my first brush with death and it seemed inconsequential. When forced to look unblinkingly into its face, most people see death as ugly, and ugly things have no place in pretty corners of the world like Fontana and Moreno Valley. The deaths of friends and schoolmates in Compton would hit home much harder and stay with me much longer.

I sometimes think about who I would be if my family had never moved from Moreno Valley. The thought often pops up when I'm speaking to a room full of inner-city schoolkids in a place like the Polo Grounds projects in Harlem, New York. In a building nicknamed "the

Vietnam Building" for the gang warfare that occurs there, I can see and feel the effect of my words. I'm talking their experiences, because I've walked in their hand-me-down sneakers and felt their one-meal-a-day hunger. But it's the kids in that auditorium at Sugar Hill who may need to hear my words just as much. That's because change starts with an understanding that doesn't come out of a book or a newspaper. If you want people to understand and embrace social issues as *their* issues—to act on those issues—you need to make those issues personal, make them tangible. Believe me, I know that these issues are easy to ignore. Insulate a house well enough and you'll never notice whether it's hot or cold outside. And you won't care. I know that, sooner or later, if anything is going to change in society, it's the kids in Sugar Hill's classrooms—and the parents at the PTA meetings—who will need to take my truth to heart. I will have to reach them as well.

Had I stayed there, grown to a man in Moreno Valley or someplace like it, I would have remained insulated. I would have had a more traditional upbringing. I might have been passionate about something, but not necessarily education for those in poverty. Maybe I would have gone into investment banking or consulting. I wouldn't have collected bottles and cans from trash bins to help pay for groceries and youth football; my first job would have been at sixteen so I could have money for clothes and gas for the car I would have been given. I might not have dreadlocks and I wouldn't know Snoop Dogg, and I would have worried less about those left behind. Compton, Harlem, Chicago, Watts—those would be place-names, vague ideas, not realities.

Instead, we left. It was perhaps the most traumatic event of my young life, even considering what would come later. But we could not stay there. Not because of racism or a lack of money. No, we had to leave because of my father.

When anyone abuses his role, whether it's a father or husband, a coach, priest, or politician, it's like someone poisoning the source of water for a massive river. The poison will now flow from the source all the way down to the smallest tributary stream. This type of poison can damage the ecosystem and everything that depends on the river, sometimes permanently. Abusers live in fear that others will see the blackness they see when they look in the mirror. I know now that my father had horrible demons. He was haunted by terrible ghosts of abuse, neglect, and abandonment as a child. My mom believes he suffers from mental illness, and maybe she's right. I have to think that his need to dominate, that abusiveness, comes from somewhere deep, from when he was young. It would eventually lead him down the darkest of paths. But first, it led my mother away from him.

Kids are oblivious. Whatever is happening around them is "the normal" until they are old enough to know anything different. I think back and what I remember is a happy childhood in Fontana and Moreno Valley. That big house and all the things we had—dirt bikes, a full refrigerator, the Sega Dreamcast, and the big-screen Mitsubishi TV. The luxury and ease of it all. My sister and brother there with me. But behind these peaceful domestic scenes, my mother was made to suffer, and the big house in Fontana was a prison to her. Once, when my dad was heading to work before a trip out of town, my mom asked him for some money for groceries. She was a few days away from her payday and needed a little help. He refused. So I remember a fun weekend of nights camping in the backyard, eating watermelon and hot dogs. Only later would I learn that those hot dogs and watermelon were all the food we had left in the kitchen, and the backyard camping adventure was my mom's way of turning a negative situation into a positive experience in light of the fact that our food was scarce. It was a way for her to ensure my sister and I didn't catch on to what was happening.

When she took us to visit her mother (she never went alone, because my father let her know that he "wasn't a babysitter"), my father would demand that she check in several times a day. He dictated how much she spent on groceries and he had to approve any money she spent on herself, even though she brought in more money than he did. If she did anything to displease him, broke any of his many, many rules, he would rage. He never hit her, but he would punch walls by her head and broke furniture many times. And even though he didn't hit her, she feared that he could, at any time. The older we got, the more she worried that she wouldn't be able to protect us from him, that he would get to us with his rage, possibly even hurt one of us.

To hear her tell it, there was no grand master plan to leave. Her sister had been urging her to get out of the relationship for a long time. My father had once pulled a gun on one of my auntie's boyfriends, so there was no love lost between him and his in-laws. Adults around her could see the damage he was doing, the abuser he was. Then, on October 17, 2000, the opportunity just presented itself.

My father was a Mason. The Masons were having a convention in West Covina, and he told my mother that he was going to spend the week there. On Monday he said, "Look, I'm going to be at this convention for four days. I don't want you calling me. I don't want you texting me. I don't want to hear from you. I'm going to be with my brothers, and I don't need to be bothered with you and the kids."

My mother just nodded her head, but inside the wheels were turning. It was a gift. She said, "Okay, fine. Just do me a favor, please. Once you check into the hotel, give me a call and let me know that you made it safe."

When my father got to the hotel, he called her to let her know he had checked in and that he was safe. He told her not to bother him by calling while he was away. She hung up the phone, took a breath, and started calling her family. She gathered my sister, my brother, and me, and told us, "We're going to go to Grandma's house for a while. Grab some toys you want to take."

It seemed like an adventure, like fun. There were my mom's relatives, my grandma and my aunties and other people, and this bright orange U-Haul truck. We regularly went to my grandma's on weekends, so it didn't seem that unusual, except that the adults were putting a bed, a dresser, and our TV in the truck and piling our clothes in my mom's forest-green Ford Explorer. My aunt drove my mom's midnight-green Infiniti behind us, a car that would be sold a few years later to make ends meet.

We drove away from the beige-and-brown Moreno Valley house on Odessa Drive on a warm October evening. It would be the last time I would see that house.

We settled in at my grandma's house on the border of Compton and Carson. Though it was already packed with a collection of aunts, uncles, and cousins, my mom felt that having us around family would be the safest option away from my dad. We set up my mom's California King–size bed in one of the bedrooms, and we all slept in the bed together. For the first few weeks, my mom did everything she could to keep as much normality in our lives as possible. Before leaving, she had been working part-time so that she could study for law school. But she had to flee from her job for her own safety and that of her children. We took a heavy financial hit as a result. My mom had saved up a few thousand dollars that would help us get by, but the money slowly dwindled without any income from my dad, the loss of her part-time job, and law school tuition. She was attending law school during the day by that time, and she drove Mi and me back to Sugar Hill Elementary every morning on her way to school. But she soon got to a point where she had to deal with the reality of living in Compton. She simply couldn't continue to make the nearly hour-and-a-half commute to keep us in Sugar Hill, so she enrolled us at the nearby elementary school, about six blocks from my grandma's house.

I still didn't completely understand what was happening. When my mom took me to the school to sign me up and explained I would be going there instead of Sugar Hill, I trusted her that there was a good reason. I didn't ask why I was switching schools. It was kind of cool and novel at first. The school looked very different from Sugar Hill, more beat up, and it seemed a little edgy and exciting. Then I sat in one of the classrooms and man, it was different. In a really bad way. I came home scared.

Attending this new elementary school was the tipping point, when I realized that everything we were doing, everything we were going through, wasn't temporary. It was the new reality, and my world was upside down.

Classes at my new school were a shocking change from Sugar Hill, as different as night and day. My first-grade class didn't sit in chairs, as we had at Sugar Hill. Instead, it was more like a preschool class. In place of chairs, there was a mat with colored squares covering the floor. Each child sat on a square, and it seemed like the main goal of my teacher was to keep the kids quiet and behaved. The teaching was far below anything I had experienced at Sugar Hill. Most of the students in Moreno Valley came into school already able to read. But in this first-grade class, nearly half the kids were illiterate. And the teacher did little to remedy that situation. She was a short, top-heavy woman who dressed every day in the same red sweater and black pants, her "twisty" dreadlocks her only nod to the fashion of Compton. She wasn't nasty or bitter; she was just an entirely disinterested, unequipped, and perhaps unqualified teacher. Many of those kids who came into her first-grade classroom unable to read would, at the end of the year, be unceremoniously passed on to second grade, still illiterate.

The lessons I learned were no longer academic; they were about how things worked—or didn't—at the school. One day when my teacher was out sick, we had a substitute teacher from the special education department. She began asking the class questions: if we knew what something was, or how to spell certain things.

"Does anybody know 'encyclopedia'?"

My hand shot up, and then, before she could even acknowledge me, I spelled the word. Confident and fast, as we had done at Sugar Hill.

The substitute sneered at me. "What, you think you're smart?"

"No." It seemed, by her tone, like the answer she wanted.

"You think you know stuff?"

Now I was a little confused. She was really making it sound like I had done something wrong. "Well, I know some things."

"Well, guess what. You don't know everything."

I was hurt. I was getting torn down for something I would have been praised for at Sugar Hill. The rules had changed, but now they didn't make any sense. You were supposed to be in school but not show any enthusiasm or knowledge? And the nasty way the teacher had said it cut me to the core. I sat quietly, hiding my tears. I felt completely belittled and alone.

I had butted up against one of the rules in the hood: don't stand out too much. If you appear exceptional in any way, outside of sports and entertainment, people will tear you down. Teachers did it. Other kids did it. Gangbangers and even cops did it. People make sure you know your "place." Sometimes you even keep yourself in check, making sure that your priorities are kept in line with the people around you. It can be scary when someone takes an alternative path to success, especially through education. Especially a young black kid. It can make others feel smaller in the difficulties of their lives.

Just the same, I knew I had to excel. Because I transferred to my new school in the middle of a semester, I wasn't able to take the entrance exams for placement in the higher-level classes. So I was placed in the lowest "track" in school—that level of kids the school system essentially writes off. Many elementary schools in Los Angeles Unified School District had a track system based on test scores from when students were six years old. A perverse logic was at work: rather than give low performers the help and attention they needed, they were grouped in larger classes, with less resources, and taught by the least capable teachers. It was a self-fulfilling prophecy of failure. For the remainder of their schooling, the students were held accountable for their academic performance at six years old, hostages of the lower track all the way through twelfth grade.

Schools like mine have "magnet" tracks, with better teachers and newer books. Much of your future depends on which track they slot you into as a six-year-old. I had heard a rumor that private prisons determine how many facilities they want to build for the future based on third-grade test scores in the track system. At the time, I didn't understand the word *private*, but I knew for a fact that I never wanted to go to prison.

My first-grade year at my new school was horrible. I had a tough transition. The first conversation I ever engaged in on the schoolyard was with some kids in my class who were talking about what they would do when they went to prison one day.

"When I go to prison, Imma become a Crip automatically. They gon' have my back."

"For me, Imma pretend to be a Muslim. I heard they leave you alone if you're religious."

When it came my turn to say what I would do when I went to prison one day, I didn't know how to respond. I had never thought of going to prison until that point.

In first grade, I got into at least one fight per week. I was singled out by other kids because I had not fully adapted to life in the hood yet. My mom cut my hair, and she didn't know how to edge me up the way my dad did, so she left my hairline looking crazy. At recess kids would clown me for my uneven taper or for my mom pushing my hairline back too far. Unbeknownst to me, it was also uncool to wear your pants at the waistline, exposing your socks. Kids called it "flooding" or wearing "high-waters." They would say, "Your hairline looks like my grampa's," or "Why are your pants so high? You about to go crush some grapes?"

When I would report this to my teacher or the recess supervisors, I was told not to let anyone pick on me. So I responded to their advice by putting my chubby little hands on anyone any time they had something funny to say about me. I hated fighting. I also hated that my teacher didn't seem to care about my well-being, let alone my education. At six, I began entertaining ideas of not going to school anymore. But there was Mom. The only bright spot from my first-grade year was that my mom graduated from law school in May. I saw my only superhero walk across the stage with a pride, honor, and esteem that I had never seen in human form. That lit a fire under me again, underlining my feeling that education was important indeed. I didn't know how I was going to do it, but I wanted better for myself. I wanted to at least be in a magnet program, in a higher track.

I saw my opportunity when my second-grade teacher announced there would be a school-wide spelling bee. I somehow convinced myself that after the school saw my performance in the spelling bee, they would move me up to a magnet program automatically. Each class would hold its own bee, and the winners would compete in front of the whole school. We were given a packet of sixty sheets containing potential words. For three months I studied those sheets like they were scripture. If the power was out in the house, I'd study them by flashlight or even by candlelight. To my surprise, I won our classroom spelling bee easily.

On the day of the school-wide competition, I put on a dark green turtleneck and fake black glasses, thinking they made me look like Harry Potter. I didn't own a Harry Potter book and had never read one. But I thought Harry Potter looked smart. People were surprised to see me up there with all the kids who had parents that fought to get them into the magnet program. The entire school filled the auditorium and there was an air of excitement. I was ready and in the zone.

We went around and around, people falling out on a regular basis. Some would start crying; others would just leave the stage nonchalantly, as if it were nothing. Perhaps for them it was. Many of the magnet kids had stable home lives, two parents, and not a lot of worries. They didn't have a lot riding on a spelling bee, but I convinced myself that if I could win it, I could make my mark and it would lead to great things.

Before I even realized it, there were only two people left on stage, me and a magnet student named Tyra. I was asked to spell "building." Easy. I said, "Building . . . *b*, *i* . . ." I stopped. I knew right away what I had done. I put my hand on my head, stunned. I walked back to my seat with tears welling in my eyes. Tyra spelled it right without hesitation. For me, it was such a simple word to lose on. It was a pivotal moment in my young life.

I had my face in my hands when the kid next to me tapped me on the shoulder. They called me back up onstage to receive my trophy, and then I realized I had won second place. It wasn't first, but I had done well. I had never won anything before. I had an epiphany, right there. I realized that if I applied myself as I had for the spelling bee, and if I had an opportunity to apply that hard work, I would be able to manifest something positive. I might not make my goal, but I would realize something good from it. Though my resources were limited, I hoped for more opportunities like the spelling bee to come along. The experience gave me a work ethic that I could trust in regardless of what was going on around me in the hood. That second-place trophy in the second-grade spelling bee remains, for me, the most important accomplishment of my life. That trophy is what set the tone.

I think that simple victory actually did lead me further than I had expected. The next school year, someone looked at my records, considered what I had done, and placed me in the magnet program. It would ultimately open doors to a better middle school, which in turn led to a stellar high school and beyond. Like dominoes falling in a row. I traced that all back to the work I put in studying for a simple little spelling bee. But I have to think back to those other kids who were left behind in the lower tracks. The other kids who didn't make it to the spelling bee. The kids who didn't win a trophy. Some I've never heard of again, and some I've seen in handcuffs on the news.

Of course, there were other more bitter lessons. Compton was the start of a very different type of education for me. When I came home from school, I no longer asked the questions of innocence, questions like, “Why is the sky blue?” or “Why is the grass green?” I came home one day after having overheard some of my classmates talking about the candlelight vigil on the center-divider that stood across the street from their house, and what might have happened on the scene. I asked my mom, “Mom, what’s a Crip?”

Much of what I had to deal with and learn were blank spaces that, in any young man’s life, a male role model would have normally filled in. But I didn’t have one. We were completely cut off from my father because my mother had gotten a restraining order. She was concerned he might confront her and get violent. We didn’t see him, we didn’t talk to him on the phone, and we didn’t even talk about him. Hard as that was, time and subsequent events would prove how good my mother’s judgment had been.

I would learn as much from the street, from the brutality born of poverty and fear, as I would in any classroom. From that young age, I realized that Compton was abnormal, an outsider society. Everyone there had, in one way or another, been marginalized. Later I would understand that if I were ever to change that place and places like it, I’d have to use to my advantage all the lessons

Compton taught me. I'd have to be an example of why the perception of places like Compton should not define the people who live there. I'd also have to seek out a platform that would allow me to reach people outside Compton. Changes can come from the people in Compton, but large-scale change in similar communities all over the country would take a collective effort to bring about. The platform I would find would be education and football. Getting there would involve using my raw intellect, survival skills, street smarts, hard work, and faith in things unseen. But in a place like Compton, most of the time, that's not enough.

2

QUESTION: *"Give us a better understanding of what your inner drive is like and how you got to where you are."*

By 2004 I was becoming used to things being different from how they had been. I didn't have my own room anymore. My mom didn't have her own house. There were no cupboards full of Cap'n Crunch or Cookie Crisp. The refrigerator was empty, except for a bottle of mustard and a box of baking soda. The nights weren't quiet and still. There was a lot of gunfire. We always heard sirens several times during the night and early morning. My mom slept on the outside edge of the king-size bed she shared with Mi, Chase, and me, because Mom got up first. She took the longest to get ready.

Chase slept scrunched in the middle, and I was up against the wall. Everybody was squeezed for space. My sister was the smart one. When we first moved to that overcrowded, decrepit three-bedroom house off Avalon Boulevard, she staked out the space across the foot of the bed, defining it with her ragged old gray sleeping bag. Chase and I were still short enough that our feet didn't kick her, and nobody rolled over on her in the middle of the night. Mi had some good sense.

There was no point in complaining, but I didn't like being against the wall. I learned to sleep through the sounds of gunshots, but I could hear rats and cockroaches scurrying behind the cracked plaster on and off all night. The squeaks and scurries made it sound like the rats and roaches were having a little war of their own. I often woke up with something crawling across my face, batting it off in semiconscious panic. If I ever dropped something between the wall and the bed, I would wait until daytime to get it, when I could see what was down there. I was afraid to put my hand by the plaster and get bitten by something.

When Mom got up, everyone got up. Share a bed with four people and any time anyone moves, it wakes everybody. First thing every morning, Mom made sure our school uniforms—navy-blue khakis and polo shirts—were waiting on hangers. Like all the inner-city elementary schools in Los Angeles Unified School District, my elementary school required this basic uniform. It was their way of making sure no kid wound up ridiculed because his parents couldn't afford clothes. To accommodate kids who wanted to express themselves through their clothing, Fridays were free-dress days, when we were allowed to wear something other than the basic uniform. I hated free-dress Fridays. My only free-dress outfit was a pair of patchwork jeans, a knockoff white-and-green Ricky Williams Dolphins Jersey, and a pair of Shaquille O'Neal shoes from Payless. I didn't mind wearing the school uniform because it meant that no one at school could clown me for my lack of gear. And the uniform worked for my mom, because she wanted us to look "decent and in order" anytime we left the house, and because my father had cut off contact and had failed to pay child support, she had to make do on a tight budget.

We got dressed, three sleepy little kids with only the faint morning light to guide us. If we wanted electricity in our part of the house, we had to run an orange extension cord from the only working outlet on the other side of the house. But it always overloaded the circuit and flipped the breaker, so mostly we just did without power or lights. You learn to move around in the dark without bumping into things or each other. Because it was dark anyway, I would just do it with my eyes closed to test my memory skills.

When my mom was dressed and ready, we hustled out. We moved quick, not even thinking about if we were hungry or not. There was usually nothing to eat for breakfast.

Sometimes my grandma, my auntie Cyndi, or my uncle Christian—each of whom also lived in the house—would get themselves takeout, big helpings of Chinese food or a takeaway box of soul food. Being a little kid and not knowing any better, I would ask, "Can I eat your leftovers?"

"Nope, I'm gonna eat them later. You can't have those leftovers." In Compton, people felt that they had to protect what little they could scrape out for themselves. I knew they loved me. I just assumed that they didn't realize how hungry I truly was. Because she and my auntie and uncle never engaged in physical activity and only ate twice a day, my grandma thought that I was greedy for expecting three meals a day. I started to think she was right. I also thought that it was important to make sure that all the girls in the house ate first and ate sufficiently. It was expected that my brother and I would eat last or not at all for the sake of the girls, since we were the "men of the house." I never for one second questioned the food hierarchy.

Instead of complaining, Chase and I made a two-day rule: if someone didn't eat their leftovers within two days, the food was ours. I developed a tough stomach, letting me pick through food with partial rot and mold. Even then it was a gamble. The refrigerator didn't work very well, and sometimes the leftovers went truly bad. I only found out when that happened when I would suddenly throw up in the boy's bathroom at school. I didn't like throwing up at any time, but it was even worse in that dirty room with its cracked tile, broken mirror, and stale pee smell. So I never counted on breakfast.

In time, Mom started dropping us off at Miss Pam's on her way to work. Miss Pam was a friend of a friend of my mom's, a black woman, tall and substantial. She was in her midthirties with long black hair and deep green eyes. She ran a day care out of her house. We would have cereal with her, and then she would drive us to school and pick us up when we got out. I loved the cereal and other meals that we ate at Miss Pam's. Mom called her our "sitter." My mom didn't use Miss Pam because we couldn't take care of ourselves and each other; she did it because she didn't want us walking to school.

We lived in a gang neighborhood, and bangers were everywhere. She didn't want the violence going on around us to infect our view of humanity. My mom never gave into that place or our circumstances. She was a constant example to us of what power, focus, and drive looked like in action. She was always styling in a sharp gray pinstripe or navy-blue skirt suit when she went to work. She stood perfectly straight, making the most of the fact that she was nearly six feet tall. Her beautiful wavy hair was brushed to a shine. Her makeup was perfect. After she graduated from law school, Mom had gotten a job at a law firm doing client intake consultations and preparing things like interrogatories, pleadings, and motions. The firm was in a clean, upscale, nicely decorated office building in the heart of the South Bay area of Los Angeles. I'm positive that everyone in that office thought she went home at night to Brentwood or Sherman Oaks. They would probably have been shocked to discover that she commuted an hour back to Compton to sleep four to a bed with her children.

She was driven to move beyond our situation, to get us out of a house we shared with ten relatives—my grandma, aunties, uncles, cousins, and occasionally family friends. Many family members used my grandma's house as transitional housing when life hit them hard and there was nowhere else to go. There was a time where as few as five people lived in Grandma's house, and there was a time where as many as fourteen lived there. Even with the money my mom started earning after law school, she couldn't afford to uproot us again and move us to another place.

My mom also lived under the constant threat of danger from my dad. After she left him disturbing things began to happen to her—her gas was siphoned, and her tires were slashed. More than once my mom got into her forest-green Ford Explorer to head to work only to find a dead kitten that had been stuffed into a sock, sitting on the hood of her car. My mother believed my father was the culprit, and she obtained a restraining order that cited these terrifying threats. One morning, as my grandmother took out the trash, I looked through the living room window to watch her. She bent down to pick something up off the porch. I focused my gaze only to realize that she had picked up a dead kitten with what looked like a bullet pushed into the front of its head. Terror coursed through my body.

Without flinching, my grandma came back into the

house and put single garlic cloves in four different socks. She then nailed these socks over most of the doors in the house. Placing garlic over doorways is a practice used by Afro-Latina and Afro-Caribbean people in places like Honduras and Belize to ward off evil spirits. My grandma sat down on the dining room couch. She opened her Bible, said a prayer, and then went on about her day. My mom responded to my father's terrorism in a similarly unwavering way. She kept moving on. Neither violence nor poverty would quell her desire for a better life for her children. She was determined every day that we focus not on where we were but where we were meant to go. She told us, "We may live in the hood, but that does not mean that the hood has to live in us."

She taught us both by how she acted and by the words she preached. She reminded me often, "When you give God your absolute best, he will bless it and then give it back to you." I knew that meant that when you are in agreement with the Lord, the more you put your faith to work in something, the more you confront adversity, the more powerfully God will see you through your storm.

My personal drive was always fueled by hunger. Not for food. There wasn't enough food to go around, and there was nothing I could do about that. But there are other worse hungers. Hunger for love, for safety and security. The worst, though, is to starve for hope. That is the worst kind of hunger. That's the hunger I could do something about, and it's the hunger that drives me even now. I feast on hope. It carries me forward. See, any hunger can make you despair, can make you quit. Or it can make you a hunter. I came to realize in the hood that as much as it hurt, I could go without food. But I was damned if I was going without hope. And I mean that literally—without hope, I was doomed. I would always hunt for hope in whatever I did. Like many Christians, my mom saw our situation as an opportunity to rely on God. She never for a minute doubted that God would reward the hunters of hope. That was my drive—the hunger of a hunter for hope. I owed a good part of that to my mom. Not only because she was a shining example of a strong, driven woman but also because at her lowest point, I discovered my own drive and strength.

Things changed again when my mom got sick. By that point, we had gotten into a good routine, but her illness changed that. It started with her having less energy, moving slower, and being distracted. She had always made a point of asking us what homework we had and what was due next. From kindergarten on, she had drilled into us that homework equaled success. The more you brought home and the more you completed, the better you would do. She wanted to know everything that happened at school, what we learned each day. And with Mom, it wasn't just the "what," but the "who."

"Who is Angela Davis?"

"Who is Nat Turner?"

"Who is Harriet Tubman? Medgar Evers? Fred Hampton?"

She painted history for us through all the "who's." These figures were object lessons, too, people who had fought much greater challenges than we faced. She treated everything as an educational opportunity, even movies. The pause and play button of our antiquated TV remote control was rubbed bare. When we watched movies like *The Shawshank Redemption*, it wasn't for enjoyment. She would pause the movie what seemed like every five minutes.

"Did you notice the mind-set that Red has in prison? Has he embraced his oppression?"

"What makes Andy Dufresne so different from everyone else in prison?"

"Is Andy Dufresne actually in prison?"

It inspired me that a man could be in prison in his physical body but at the same time be on the beach in Mexico in his mind. In his mind he could go places that his body could not. My mom taught me that I could do that same thing.

When my mom watched movies, she kept a notepad on hand. When we watched Lakers basketball games, she kept a homemade statistics sheet to keep up with the game and work on her intellectual sharpness. My mom knew education was the secret. It was the key to every door beyond Compton. The key to the greater world, and big rooms where big people did big things. She didn't tell us—she *taught* us when we didn't know something. She took time to explain to each of us how the world worked.

But all of a sudden, she was quiet. The condition that didn't yet have a name, or even a place, silenced her. She went to bed early and didn't stand up as straight or walk as fast. Her sickness created a hole. She was there, but more and more, she wasn't.

I realized Chase was struggling. He was now in first grade in my former teacher's class, the teacher who was little more than a disinterested babysitter. Chase and I would sit on the floor of the living room, going slowly over his homework. I sensed his frustration, the way his face scrunched up like he had smelled something bad. He didn't like homework. I tried never to be impatient. Mi was in middle school. She did her homework without being told to. Even as a third grader, I knew how important my schoolwork was. It was the future of the world to me. For Chase, though, it was a big iron ball he had to drag with him every night. So I sat with him until he was done.

Mom's health got worse bit by bit. We were little kids, so we didn't really notice until it was too obvious to ignore. By the time we got out of school for summer break, she could barely walk up the driveway in front of the house without getting winded. She would sleep even after the rest of us got up if we didn't wake her. She never complained, but we all knew something was very wrong.

For that entire summer she struggled, taking off day after day from work. She had never called in sick before. I went about my summer, thinking my mom would get better. I mean, that's what happens, right? You get sick, then you get better. It didn't dawn on me that it might not work that way. Meanwhile, we played basketball when the kids next door were around. They had the only hoop and ball in the neighborhood. We got games of street football together when there were enough kids. When there weren't, Chase and I played catch. Or I rode my beat-up rollerblades, two sizes too big, and hit targets with the football while I was moving. Good practice. When we came inside, Mom was usually lying down. It became more and more typical to see her out of energy. I kept expecting her to be back to her old self the next day. Sometimes, though, I could hear her struggling for breath. I thought to myself that I wanted to give her some of mine, to breathe for her, but I didn't know how.

September came around, and a couple weeks after I started fourth grade, she was referred to Dr. Rhaghunathan, a heart specialist in the network for the insurance my mom had from her job. I never met him, but Mom said he really knew what he was doing. He was smart and caring. Her doctor did tests and more tests. The results came back and the news wasn't good.

Cardiomyopathy. A word I had never heard before and a word I came to hate. One chamber of my mom's heart was enlarged. Another chamber had polyps, which were interfering with blood flow. She needed open-heart surgery. I didn't understand any of that when she sat us down at the rickety kitchen table that was a piece of history—it had been stolen out of a furniture store during the Watts riots. I sat across from my mom, with Mi on my left and Chase on my right. It was late but still light out, and I could feel Chase's leg bouncing up and down. I knew he wanted to be out playing basketball, like I did. We could hear our friends next door out there taking shots.

"I have something wrong with my heart. The doctors, they're going to do surgery and fix it," she told the three of us. She was calm and smiling, making it sound like everything would be fine. Like she was going in for nothing more serious than a teeth cleaning. She was her usual positive self. But that word *surgery* chilled all of us. In the hood, people usually died in surgery, because it was surgery for gunshots or stabbings, or cancer they never had the money to treat until it was too late. Surgery was never good. This was my greatest fear at nine: my mother dying. One day I would learn to make peace with people passing on to the other side. But at that moment, that fear was enough to block out the sun.

We just nodded. She paused for a beat to let us ask any questions. We didn't know what to ask. After a minute she nodded and smiled again. She struggled to get up and then went to lie down. I told Chase to go play. He shouldn't be thinking about it. I would do the worrying for both of us.

I sat there at that table under the light fixture with the missing shade, the two bare light bulbs. My mind raced. My nine-year-old imagination went wild. Open-heart surgery. I envisioned them taking her heart out of her body and putting it down on a metal table. How can you live without a heart? Even for a little while? The more I thought about it, the less likely it seemed that she could survive it. She was the glue holding us together. I got more and more anxious. I had a hard time catching my breath.

This was the purest fear. Mom was our anchor. Parents are supposed to be indestructible. If she died, what would happen to us? There was a lot to scare you in the hood. A lot of danger. In school, in parks, on the street. You were never really safe. I could avoid all that. I could run, I could dodge. I could find another way. But I couldn't outrun my mom having open-heart surgery.

At school the next day I couldn't think about anything else. It was like a humming inside my head that made it hard to pay attention in class or hear what the teacher was saying. I was so stressed that I started pulling out little hairs in the middle of my head until I had a noticeable bald spot. People thought it was from ringworm, but I knew it was from stress. I just didn't have the words to explain that at the time.

Ms. Freudenburg's chalk squeaked as she wrote out a math problem on the board. I didn't hear it because I was remembering my mom's ragged breathing, over and over again, like it was a signal. And if I could figurc it out, maybe it wouldn't be as bad as I thought it was. I looked at the math problem, but I didn't write it down. I didn't even really see it. I couldn't focus on anything. I was sleepwalking.

I always went to school hungry, but I didn't use my lunch cards from the free food program until the 10:00 a.m. break they called "nutrition." I got a snack. Then I waited until lunch at 12:30, when I would get a full meal. I usually ate every bit of it as quick as I could, then I would ask my fellow classmates if they were going to eat all of their food. That day at lunch, though, I stared at my green beans and meatloaf as they got cold. I sat as far away from anyone as I could. The sounds of the cafeteria were mocking me. They were happy sounds. Laughing, shouting, the banging of plastic lunch trays on sticky cafeteria tables. I just wanted some quiet time to deal with the fear. I wished that someone could feel what I was going through. I needed to convince myself, somehow, that my mom would be okay.

One of my boys, Christian Thomas, knew something was wrong. If you didn't eat in the hood, you had to be really sick. He came over to the table and sat down across from me. Chris was one of my best friends and a cool kid.

He could freestyle rap original bars without even thinking about it, and he was a good dancer, funny, and a great basketball player. I said to him, "Could we talk?"

"Sure."

"Man, my mom is going in for open-heart surgery and I'm scared she's not going to make it."

Chris knew exactly what that meant. He lived in Compton, in this place with beautiful people and unfortunate circumstances. He knew the rules and reality as well as I did. So I didn't have to say anything more. The fear was as real and substantial as if I had handed it to him. Like a rock, he could feel it, and hold it, and look at it. I started crying. Chris cried with me. Then he said, "Let's pray."

So we bowed our heads and prayed together. Two young boys with nothing much more to hold on to than the mysterious workings of a God they barely knew but who knew them very well. We prayed for my mom, and maybe for other things too. My mom had held on to her faith in God through all that had happened, and she had taught us to hold tight to that faith too. Where I'm from, you don't blame God, you thank God. God has a plan. But it is okay to ask for help.

"Please, Jesus, help us. Please. Save my mom."

I was just growing into my faith. I had been baptized the spring before at Southside Church of Christ. Located in South Central Los Angeles, the church was a bright spot in a concrete wasteland, standing upright in the middle of a worn-out stretch of inner-city blocks full of flimsy, scarred warehouses and shabby, stucco apartment buildings. It was a brick and brown-wood building with burgundy accents, a peaked roof, and many white crosses on the front. It took up a full city block. Across from it stood Silver Dollar Liquor, on the left-hand side as you drove down the street. Inside, the store was walled off in thick, bulletproof Plexiglas. There was a little slot where people swapped money for bottles. It was the physical representation of the concept "get right or get left." It was a reminder of the stark choices people face in Compton. To most of us, it was just that simple. The wrong choice versus the right choice, everywhere you turned.

I sat in those pews and listened closely to our pastor. I had already heard enough and seen enough to know that no matter how kind God was, bad things sometimes happened to good people. I was, at nine, aware that everyone died, and that life was very fragile. I had already known other kids—just children—caught in the crossfire of gang violence. Shot in the back or the head by a bullet that was aimed at someone else. A little kid, lying sprawled on a sidewalk, staring up somewhere beyond the sky, bleeding to death before the cops could clear the way for the paramedics. I knew a fifth grader named Christopher who survived being shot in the back while playing on the playground in the after-school program. The after-school program was supposed to be a safe haven for kids to stay out of harm's way. It was run by Mr. R, a tall Native American who wore a long braid down his back. A gangster named Butters hopped the fence into the elementary schoolyard and tried to rob Mr. R of his Air Jordan 18s. Mr. R took off running for his life once Butters flashed the pistol hidden at his waistline. Butters responded by letting off several shots in Mr. R's direction, missing his target but hitting Christopher, who was standing in the hallway. He had just hugged his teacher and walked out of a classroom. We turned on the TV and, to our disappointment, the local news stations didn't even cover what had happened. Just another black body that the world didn't care about.

Sometimes I battled with the notion that God overlooked the hood. It could be easy to get angry at God, especially at moments when you were going through tough times. That wasn't my mother's faith. She prided herself in becoming tougher during tough times. It was just the fear trying to shake your faith. I had already learned that you couldn't let fear rule you or you would never get anywhere. You had to turn your tests into testimonies.

One day, we had gone to Kmart to pick up a shirt for school because I'd worn out the two I had. I found a beat-up religious comic book laying in the parking lot. It was the story of Jesus' life. I must have read that comic book twenty times, front to back, that same day. I was inspired by reading that the Savior I served specialized in healing and miracles. The brightly colored panels on each page told a condensed history of Jesus as a healer. He healed a cripple, who got up and walked, and cured another man of leprosy. The images jumped off the pages at me. A man who walked around performing miracles.

I prayed again and again to God to heal my mom, too, to help her survive her surgery.

After getting the news in September, my mom started getting her affairs in order. She scheduled the surgery for March. She drafted a will and had conversations with her sisters and brothers about who would take care of us in the event she didn't make it. Money got tighter and tighter leading up to December. That year, I learned how beautiful Christmas trees could be without presents under them. I slowly started to see my hero head to ground zero. Mom went from divorcing my dad to save her children's lives to being on the verge of losing her own.

That spring, a week before the operation, she stopped going to work. She didn't get up first and she didn't dress in her business clothes. She no longer had the energy to drive us to Miss Pam's or anywhere. For the first time since we moved from Moreno Valley, we all started walking to school. Of all the changes in my young life, this was the biggest. Mi was in middle school and she had a ride. But Chase and I had a riskier path to travel.

Even in the light of day, Compton was a dangerous

place. The most direct way to our school took Chase and me through the heart of a hood that didn't welcome school dreams. We passed modest one-story houses that had probably been nice little homes fifty years before. The windows were protected with thick black iron bars, and most of the fences were topped with pointed spikes. Sometimes an old drunk would be sitting in the middle of a front yard, chilling in a crumpled easy chair. He would give us a mean stare as we walked by. Muscle-bound pit bulls occasionally threw themselves against the fences, snarling at the two of us, as angry as if we had stolen their food.

Fences, bars, and dogs. And none of these houses had anything worth stealing. Many of the yards were littered with junk, broken toys, and stuff not even the Salvation Army wanted. Once in a while we passed a large, dried bloodstain on the sidewalk. We walked around it, avoiding it like it was bad luck.

You had to cluster up with a lot of other schoolkids for the walk through the neighborhood. The Bloods looked at us like wolves do sheep. We had rules to guide us: You walked as fast as you could without running. You kept your eyes down, and if anyone said anything to you, you pretended you didn't hear and just walked faster. We looked at our shoes, stayed tight together, and wondered why it seemed to take so long to get to our destination.

One day I was walking with my brother and some friends past an open garage. About ten gang members were inside lifting weights, smoking weed, poppin' pills, and drinking from red Solo cups full of purple "sizzurp," a mixture of prescription promethazine and codeine cut with Sprite. I never judged the people who used drugs. I just assumed that the pain they'd probably gone through growing up must have made the pills easier to digest. They called us over to the garage. I wanted to take off running, but I knew that if I ran from them, I would still have to walk past this house the next day at the exact same time. You can't run from your problems in the hood. Also, I didn't want to leave Chase in the dust, because he was smaller and slower than me. So I walked over to see what they wanted. I was scared.

They asked, "Do any one of y'all little niggas wanna get put on the hood?"

That was gang jargon for being initiated into the set, or the gang.

Luckily I had my football with me. I always carried it because I loved to toss it around while I walked, and I knew it would provide me safety from gangs. Everyone respected sports.

So I said, "Nah, I just wanna play ball."

They said, "Respect, respect, go 'head then."

But to my surprise, one of my good friends actually did want to get put on the hood. He walked into the garage and stayed there as we left to walk back home. I haven't heard from him since that day. They recruited young kids to join the gang because the kids wouldn't do much time if they got caught, and would be too scared to point out who put them up to it. Like a lot of people, the Bloods thought kids in Compton were disposable.

Where I'm from, kids come to value shortcuts and escape routes. Chase and I took different ways to school on different days, depending on which I thought would be the safest. The first rule was to avoid streets whenever possible. It was just too easy to get caught walking parallel to two adults arguing and end up in a drive-by shooting. So we jumped fences into alleys and skirted along people's backyards. Sometimes it meant it was twice as far to get to school, but we usually avoided the local park and stayed clear of the gang members and the violence that rolled with them.

On the morning of March 2, 2005, the sun was shining as it always did in Southern California. There was no breeze, and the streets were quiet. But it was no ordinary day. My mom kissed each one of us on the face as we left for school. She straightened my collar and said, "You take good care of your brother, okay?" I told her I would. Then we left for school, and Auntie Cyndi drove my mother to the hospital. She checked in, went up two floors, and was prepped for surgery. That night, as I helped Chase with his homework and tried not to think about the hunger that seemed like a real, living thing trying to chew its way out of my stomach, my auntie called the hospital and checked on my mom. She told us, "Your mom is going to be fine. The surgery went real good."

We couldn't visit her because there was nobody to drive us. But I felt better knowing that she was through the worst of it. Or so I thought.

I should have known, should have figured out, that you aren't safe even in hospitals. In recovery, in a cardiac intensive care unit room, my mom lay doped up. When they operate for as long and as much as they did on my mom, they keep the patient on morphine because the trauma and healing causes so much pain. Even though she was in a drug fog, my mom realized everything that was happening when a male night nurse slipped into her room, turned up her morphine to keep her from moving or crying out, and then raped her. He did it again and again. Sometimes she was knocked out entirely. When she was awake, she was terrified of what the nurse might do if she told anyone. He was an evil person. What was to stop him from cranking up the morphine all the way and killing her?

I learned all that later. All I knew is that while she was in the hospital our bed seemed weird with just Mi, Chase, and me in it. My mother was a powerful presence. She never moped around or felt sorry for herself. She was always our pillar, and our lives felt shaky without that support. Now it fell to me to make sure our school uniforms were hung up and ready for the next day.

Night after night, I tackled my homework and then

helped Chase get through his. We ate whatever we could. Sometimes I saved a little food from lunch and brought it home. Most times, though, I was too hungry in the middle of the day and the lunch tray was as clean after I ate as it was before I was served. Every now and again my grandma put some pork and beans and sliced wieners on the stove, and we would wolf it down while it was still hot enough to burn our mouths.

I thought about my mom every hour of the day. We had never been separated. The hospital was a mystery. I had never been in one. The closest I had ever come to a hospital was watching EMTs load a shooting victim into an ambulance. I imagined it was like how I'd seen it in the movies, machines beeping and whirring. Harsh lighting. All kinds of plastic tubes everywhere. I tried not to think too much about it, because the thought of her unconscious in a hospital bed hooked up to a bunch of machines really disturbed me. In my imagination, it looked too much like she was dead.

My childish mind thought that with the surgery behind her, my mom would come home good as new. She would be standing tall, combing my sister's hair, asking Chase how he was doing with his reading, and telling me to wash up for church. About a week after the surgery, my auntie Cyndi picked my mom up from the hospital and drove her home. I was shocked—we all were—when she finally struggled through the door. She looked worse than when she had gone into the hospital. Her skin was tinged gray, her beautiful hair a tangled mess. It was all she could do to shuffle to the couch; she didn't even have the energy to hug us. She didn't look well, but there was something else I couldn't figure out. Something inside, like her flame had gone out. She just wasn't the mom I knew. She looked like a shell of that woman.

I was just glad to have her home. I told myself that this must be normal after open-heart surgery. She was alive. I gave thanks to God. But Chase was brutally honest.

"What's wrong with Mom?"

"That's how you look after surgery."

"You sure? Because she looks worse than before."

I decided it was all going to take care of itself. In the meantime, I had to keep being the man of the house. Every morning I woke up first, which got Mi and Chase going. I made sure Chase had all his schoolwork because he forgot things when he was tired. Mi took care of herself and made sure her schoolwork was on point. I mentally checked that we all looked decent and in order before leaving the house.

Still, I found ways to be a boy. Kids are kids, even in the hood. You just had to be creative. While our walking to school came to an end after Christmas break, we would often find mushroomed lumps of bullets in the gutter. We assumed that the bullets came from the inner-city tradition of people stepping outside to fire a few rounds into the air at midnight on New Year's Eve. In reality, the bullets that had mushroomed probably came from more sinister events. We collected them. Then, when we got home, we would play our version of marbles with those spent rounds. I liked the dull clinking sound they made when you flicked one into another. We gave different points to different calibers.

We tried to have fun as we figured out the best ways to get to and from school at different times. These strange, indirect routes became normal. Sometimes we raced each other from one safe spot to another. We made believe someone was trying to spy on us. Even dodging trouble could be made into a game. But in the inner city you could never be a kid for long; you slipped one kind of danger only to run into another.

One day Chase, my cousin Lorne, and I got out of school and headed toward our favorite shortcut, which meant jumping a wall three blocks from school. Lorne jumped over by himself. I hoisted Chase over, since he couldn't jump high enough yet. Chase and Lorne were on the other side, and I had just thrown over my backpack when a loud siren *whoop-whooped* behind me. Two white cops in a cruiser, lights flashing, pulled up. They got out of the car, looking angry, and made a show of walking toward me with their hands resting on their belts, over a billy club on one side and gun butt on the other. The mumble of a police radio filled the air. I had never had anything to do with the police. Before that moment, I had never even talked to a cop.

"What are you doing here?"

Even to a nine-year-old, it seemed like a silly question. It was just past two thirty, when school let out. We could see the school from where we were standing. I was in the same navy-blue khaki pants and button-down blue shirt that dozens of kids were wearing, along with a black-and-red hoodie. They filled the streets around us.

"I'm just going home."

"You have any drugs on you?"

"No."

"Weapons?"

"No."

"Keep your hands where I can see them," said the younger of the two. He was big and muscular. I was too scared to look at his face, thinking that he might take it as a threat or a challenge. Just like with the gang members in my neighborhood, whom I was truly afraid of, I kept my eyes down.

My heart was pounding so hard that I thought the cops must be able to hear it. The older one threw me up against the brick wall, scratching my face. He kicked my feet out to each side until I was awkwardly spread-eagled. He checked my pockets, turning them inside out. Chase and Lorne took off running down the street out of fear. They wanted to get someone to help but didn't know who to go to.

The cops took my name. The older one wrote it in a black notebook. "Caylin? Spell it again."

I spelled it out. They got on the radio and made me wait twenty minutes while they saw if I was in the system. Checking a nine-year-old for outstanding warrants. These men were almost as scary to me as the gang members in the garage. The gang members were once just like me. They succumbed to the hood. The way they kill one another, I think they must have learned to hate themselves. It's self-hate in the starkest form, killing people who are going through the exact same struggle as you. In that sense, I felt like I understood them to a degree. But I couldn't predict what the cops would do. Up to that moment, I had thought of them as neighborhood superheroes who came to protect us from the bad guys. But now I didn't know what to think, or why they were treating me like one of the gang members. I thought that maybe it was the hoodie I was wearing, so I used that as an excuse for their behavior. But then I realized my hoodie had a Yu-Gi-Oh! character on it from the card game. And I was just a small nine-year-old. What danger could I have been? I was worried that they would hit me. I was even more worried that they would arrest me.

At nine, I had it in my head that the police could and would arrest you and send you to jail on a whim, for absolutely nothing. It was a hood urban legend that I had heard from the older kids for years. It had been drilled into me. A sixth-grader told me about an older brother who hadn't been around, saying, "Ah man, he got arrested. They locked him up and sent him off."

"What'd he do?"

The kid looked down at his sneakers and shook his head. "Man, he didn't do *nothing*."

The longer I stood splayed against that wall, the more I convinced myself that I was going to jail. The scratch on my face was bleeding, but I didn't dare touch it or move. I didn't want to do anything that might tip the scales and make them shoot or arrest me. Finally the younger cop came back to tell me, "Okay. Get out of here, kid." I waited until they were in their cruiser and all the way down the street before I hopped the wall and ran all the way home. From that day on I never had another childhood nightmare of monsters being under my bed or in the closet. My most intense, sweat-inducing nightmares were scenes of me going to prison.

At home, my mom lay on that ratty, worn black couch. She spent day after day sleeping or just staring up at the ragged pattern of cracks in the living room ceiling. She didn't say much. It was up to the three of us to keep things going. Mi was in charge of making sure my mom ate regularly. She made her oatmeal, or soup, or whatever she could find left over in the kitchen. She had to feed Mom like you would a baby, spoon-feeding food into her mouth. I was proud of Mi's caring hands. Chase's job was to take care of the medications. There were heart medications, and my mom had diabetes, and there were pills for the pain, and other pills to stop infection. Antibiotics.

Blood thinners. There were a lot of pills. Chase worked hard to get it all right. He gave her the blue pill and small white ones first thing in the morning. Another blue and a red one in the afternoon. More at night. He made a system of it. It made me proud to be his brother.

We kept ourselves going. The schoolwork had to get done. Twice a week I washed our school shirts. It was a big production that started with cleaning the bathtub, which everyone in the house used for cold-water baths because there wasn't any hot water. We also brushed our teeth there because the sink was broken, and we washed clothes in it because we didn't have a washer or dryer. After I scrubbed the soap-and-dirt ring out of the tub, I filled it with water and squirted a bead of liquid detergent along one seam of the pants or up the front of a shirt. I scrubbed and mixed the clothes in the water until my arms were sore. Then I emptied the tub, filled it with water again, and rinsed the clothes. If you hung them right away and were careful to smooth them out nice and flat, they dried almost like they were ironed. It was all part of looking decent and in order.

We went on like that week by week. Every day I thought, *This is the day she gets back to normal*, as I passed my mom on the couch staring up at nothing. Every day I was wrong. Those weeks became a month. Still she lay on the couch. It became clearer and clearer that something was seriously wrong. I said to myself, "She's not just sick—she's sad, really sad." It was my little-kid way of wrapping my head around the fact that she was clinically depressed and suffering from PTSD. I had never heard of mental illness up to that point in my life.

There was nowhere to turn, no one to call even if I had a phone. My grandma, aunties, and uncles all had their own problems to deal with. They loved my mom too, I thought, but they had no idea what was wrong with her, and no tools to fix it. We were in a house with more than ten people, but Mi, Chase, and me? We were all alone.

Finally, about two months after Mom came home, I realized that I had to do something. There were a lot of nine-year-old adults in my community. The hood forces kids to make adult decisions. Are you going to school even though it seems like an unlikely option for success? Are you going to sell drugs? Are you going to do drugs? Are you going to call the cops on your abusive stepfather? Are you going to join a gang and start banging? Are you going to study even though you have to stand in class because there aren't enough seats, and your textbook doesn't mention the first Iraq War, much less the second? Are you going to rob and steal to help the family get some food? What are you going to do? Each and every day, that's the question: What are you going to do?

Are you going get your mom up off that couch or just let her lie there, fading away until she becomes nothing more than a part of the furniture?

My decision, as man of our house at nine, was that I had to get her up and doing something "normal." I figured it could be anything other than letting things stay the bad way they were. I vaguely remembered a movie where a black woman washed her hair as a sign that the hard times, the worst of things, were over. I decided that the simple act of getting clean would help my mom get back to who she was. I dragged one of the wobbly wooden kitchen chairs into the bathroom and put it in the middle of the bathtub. I wrapped the chair in a black thirty-gallon trash bag. Then I stood over my mom. She looked through me as if she didn't even know I was there. I took a deep breath and gathered my courage.

"Mom, come on, you've got to get up. You got to live. We need you."

To my surprise, she seemed to really see me for the first time since she'd gotten home. She reacted. She moved to sit up like someone drugged, like someone wearing clothes too heavy and thick. She slowly, slowly, slowly stood up. I grabbed her arm and led her into the bathroom, pulling her along as she stumbled. One step at a time.

I took off her clothes. I undressed her like you would a child, and I guess that's what it was; we had to switch roles. This strong, beautiful giant of a woman, the strongest person I had ever met, needed me to be the parent right then. She had become the child, and she needed an adult to help her.

I sat her down in the chair, naked. I could see she really didn't understand what was happening. It didn't register. I filled the cracked red plastic bucket with cold water from the faucet with pliers for a handle. I stood up and poured the water over her. She made a big, loud gasp. It was the loudest noise I had heard from her in a month. The water made a satisfying pretty sound as it splashed out of the bucket all at once, running in a river down through her hair, over her face, across her broad shoulders and tracing the big angry scar from her surgery. It coated her whole body. I filled another bucket and, even though she was shivering now, I poured that one over her too. She said something that sounded like, "Oh, oh . . ."

Tears filling my eyes, I commanded my mom, "Mom, wash your hair."

I got the worn yellow bar of Dial soap and started washing her shoulders. Then I made a handful of suds and patted it on her face, legs, and arms. I could see the light start to come back into her eyes. Those eyes that glittered like diamonds, full of tears of pain and embarrassment, followed me as I just kept washing her. I started in on her hair, her beautiful hair. It had always been long and shiny and wavy. Her mother's side of the family came from Honduras, Belize, and Jamaica, and that's where she got her hair. I had never seen it this dirty or tangled. Now I could feel her body shaking with the cold. That was what I thought, anyway. But it was actually her sobbing.

And man, she cried. It shook her whole body top to bottom, like when you have so much to be sad about that it took extra big tears to cry it out. I filled the bucket again and poured more cold water over her, washing her clean.

Sometimes a shock is the best medicine. Once in a while, a person just needs something crazy to happen, something unimaginable, so that they can find their way back to normal. For my mom, it was the realization that her nine-year-old son was bathing her. Something inside her snapped hearing me say, "Wash your hair." That bright flashing light came back on in her eyes. Just like that, she was there again. She got out of the bathtub, still shivering, and dried herself. She got dressed. She started moving around and talking. The next week, she went back to work.

I can't say things got back to normal, because deep down, I knew that place was anything but normal. Even as we got our mom back, even as we went back to four to a bed and life as usual, I was so hungry. I craved the hope that would lead me out of this place. I chased hope all the way to school and brought it home again. I put hope into every pass I threw as I practiced perfect spirals in the street.

Many years later I would crave a bigger hope. A hope that Compton wasn't Compton anymore, that no teenager ever wore a red bandanna or owned a Glock 9 or felt the need to shoot someone because they were disrespected or just high. That no nine-year-old had to be an adult. I would, one day, have big hopes for this community, for all these people. Not just for Compton, but for all the people in "the struggle."

That would come later. At nine, I devoured the smaller hope that took me forward day by day. It was the hope that was rescued as I watched my mom stand tall again, walk with purpose and power, wearing her best suit and leading her kids out the door each morning. Normal, everyday hope. It was what I saw in the faithful faces of the people filling the hardwood pews around us each Sunday at Southside Church of Christ. It lit up the eyes and smiles of the other kids like me, who worked hard to earn their desks in the top track, the magnet classes at my elementary school. Those kids who would probably never be gang members or criminals or lost souls.

I found hope especially in the renewed drive I saw in my mom, because I realized I had that same drive. It lived in me just as it lived in her. It was like a secret superpower. In the weeks and months following her bath, my mom went into Super Woman mode. She went back to work, got us all to church every week, and kept busy. There was no space for her to deal with her psychological issues. She didn't process what she had gone through or the damage to her mental health. She had skipped some steps, and later she would be forced to come back and walk through them more carefully. She would file a criminal complaint.

There would be lawyers and lawsuits. But right then, she was mostly back to the mom I knew.

Hope was as essential to me as air. But I had another hunger that was getting sharper. Football. I had played football for the first time when I was four years old, and I was crazy for it from that moment. I had a knack for it too. I played in a flag football league when we lived in Fontana, and I was such a fanatic that my mom made me wear Pull-Ups during games because I wouldn't come out even for a bathroom break. I didn't want to miss a single second of the game. I wanted to win, but more than that, I wanted to play. It was the first time I found myself driven to something. And I really got after it.

For a kid growing up in a single-parent household, it was nearly impossible to get on a team. My school didn't even have a flag football team. The local youth league was in Carson, and it was expensive. The entry fee was more than $400, way more than I could ever hope to save collecting returnable cans and bottles. One Saturday, my mom drove me to Victoria Park and appealed to the league official sitting at the registration table. She explained that we couldn't afford the entry fee but that I would work tirelessly and do the league proud. She tried to describe the burning desire, the sheer hunger I had to play football. How much it meant to me. She asked if she could work out a payment plan or a reduced fee. The league, though—they didn't care. They looked at me like I was just another kid from the hood trying to get a handout. They weren't having it. *You want to play, you pay.* Those were the rules for the Carson Colts. On that day, because of the way they looked at me, I felt poor.

But a former hood kid named Calvin Broadus Jr. was about to change the rules of the game. He knew better than anyone that there were tons of kids like me: kids who didn't just want to play ball, they needed to play ball. He knew that football was one of the few positive diversions disadvantaged kids living in impoverished, inner-city neighborhoods could turn to in order to get away from gangs, poverty, trouble with law enforcement, hopelessness, and the other problems that plagued life in the hood.

Yes, Calvin knew as much as you could know about all that. See, Calvin had been there. He knew because he was at one time a member of the Rollin' 20 Crips on the east side of Long Beach, California. He dealt drugs, did drugs, and carried a gun. That was all before he became the world-famous multiplatinum rapper named Snoop Dogg. And it was long before he founded the youth football league that would bear his name. That program would be a saving grace for me, a gift from a loving God. It would be the start of my football career that, in turn, would provide me a path out of the hood.

3

QUESTION: *"What do you think about the danger of football and the brutality of the sport in terms of concussions, etc.?"*

My tackle football career began in middle school. I had wanted to play in fifth grade when I'd gotten my first taste of the prestige that players enjoy in Carson. Some kids would show up in cool blue-and-white letterman jackets and play football in the yard during lunch. They would excitedly recount the games they had just played on the weekend. These were all "middle-class" kids according to the hood definition, which just meant they all had both a mother and father at home. I envied them. They seemed to have great lives. I played pickup games with them on the playground and it was clear I was better. I wanted my letterman jacket. They knew I could play.

"Hey man, you got to play for the Carson Colts White."

"Don't listen to him—you want to join the blue. They the better Colts."

But of course, in the end, the Colts had no desire to take a kid who couldn't afford the $400 entry fee. My mom and I also felt like those Carson Colts people took youth football way too serious and were looking down at us. So I stuck to playing street football, because it was all

I could afford. Right in front of my house, light pole to light pole, with the neighborhood kids.

As much as I was fixated on football, I knew that education would be just as key to getting out of my circumstances. Unlike a lot of kids in the system, I didn't leave my choice of middle school up to chance. We were zoned for a local school, one that became infamous as a place where young kids went off the rails. It was easy to get caught up in the wrong lifestyle there. Young boys were particularly vulnerable because of the gang activity at the school, and every year a few kids got in trouble for bringing a family member's gun to class. Drugs were everywhere, and several students got pregnant each year. Kids thirteen and fourteen. It was a subpar placeholder for what a middle school should be. And I was determined not to go there.

I got my hands on a packet mailed by the district outlining how to apply for schools outside your zone. One school jumped out at me: the 32nd Street School, a University of Southern California magnet middle school. At the time, USC had two Heisman trophy winners, Reggie Bush and Matt Leinart. Every kid on the playground wanted to be Reggie Bush. USC had a legendary football program, and the idea of going to a middle school associated with the university was incredibly exciting. I talked it over with my mom, and she was supportive, encouraging me to apply. I was naive in thinking simply applying and being earnest about my desire to go there would entitle me to a place in the school. After waiting weeks with the assumption that of course I would get in, my application was denied.

My fallback was Dodson Middle School, a large school in Rancho Palos Verdes, one of the wealthiest cities in California. Dodson offered two magnet programs. The highly gifted program was at the top and included door-to-door shuttle service for each student. It sounded ideal, but I had waited too long, assuming that I would get into the USC program, so there were no slots left. Instead, I applied for the second-level magnet program that provided roughly the same educational opportunities (Dodson provided two textbooks for each subject—one to keep at home and one to keep at school), but without transportation assistance.

My mother's schedule was squeezed tight, so she could rarely afford the extra time to drive me to school. Instead, I would wake up at 5:00 and do a little bit of homework. At around 5:45, my mom would take me to the bus station to catch the 6:04 bus. That was crucial, because if I missed it I would have to take the 6:30 bus, which meant riding with all the high school students and gang members. As the smallest kid on that bus, I was an easy target.

The bus line was a learning experience in and of itself. The route ran through a patchwork of neighborhoods, from the most down-and-out places to gated communities. It was a mini-tour of what a city is, how it's put together socially and economically. At the end of the ride, I'd get off the bus and walk up the half-mile hill to school.

When I got out of school, I'd ride the bus in the opposite direction and walk home from the bus station in Gardena. Afternoons were the riskiest time in my day because gang members would be on the prowl. I hated that part of my schedule more than I can possibly describe. On any given day, anywhere along that walk, I might have to drop my backpack and take off running. There was no knowing what to expect. I'd walk slowly from the bus station, turn the corner, and then start calculating. You had to see everything from a distance and try to make the right decisions. There was only one way in and out of my neighborhood, only one street to my grandma's house, and right smack in the middle was the mini-park where the gang members hung out. That time of day, the gang members would be lounging and bored, ready for any kind of amusement. So I would have to ask myself, *Man, do I want to hop a fence early? Do I want to hop it later? Right now? Which side of the street do I walk on? If I walk opposite those guys down there, will they think I'm scared?* Because being scared just made you more of a target. *Or do I want to walk right past them and be bold?* It was a world of crucial decisions that needed to be made just to get home.

The worst was when they'd roll up on me, four guys in a car. If I saw a black 2005 Monte Carlo with twenty-two-inch rims, I knew I was in trouble. I'd try to skinny behind a tree. The bangers would slow down to walking speed, and the passenger would roll down his window and throw up his gang signs. If they didn't seem that serious, I might just stand there a second, look him straight in the face, and then keep walking. Once in a while they'd flash a gun, laughing. Everyone in the car, laughing. When that gun showed, I'd take off. Just drop my backpack and run. I didn't want anything to do with a gun. Are they going to shoot you? Maybe not, but you never know. They could be high, or maybe somebody is getting "put on" to the hood. All of sixth grade I barely carried a backpack to school. Once I was out of my mom's sight, I would leave it in a bush or just not take it at all. I saw it as an inconvenience. I was a poor student in sixth grade because I was always losing my notes and other paperwork. In the hood, schoolwork is secondary to survival.

Danger is relative. Do you leap out of a burning building and risk breaking your legs? That's the kind of logic that's at work when kids and parents in the inner city think about football. The situations I regularly faced on the street made any danger on the football field seem purely theoretical and laughable. Concussion damage in my thirties? Most boys in Compton are just looking to make it to eighteen. Many young men assume that they will die before their grandmas do. Worrying about concussions is for people who have the luxury of hypotheticals. That's why even though she was concerned about the dangers of football, my mom continued to help me find a team to play on. The Carson Colts might have been out of our reach, but my mom had other resources.

The church in underserved communities is inevitably a tight-knit network. People help each other out. Through Southside Church of Christ, Mom had struck up a friendship with a man everybody called Coach Tony. Coach Tony had a chinstrap beard and broad smile, and the husky, muscular frame of someone who had once played linebacker. He refereed football games on the weekends and aspired to be an NFL ref, like his father. He was looking to make money through refereeing, but he wanted to change young lives through coaching.

My mother told Coach Tony about our experience with the Carson Colts. He said, "You know, I'm coaching a team. Y'all should come out to a practice."

Coach Tony's team was the Southern California Falcons, part of the Snoop Youth Football League. It seemed like it might be the perfect opportunity. But my mom was still conflicted for precisely the reason the Rhodes committee would ask me about later. She knew better than anyone how much football meant to me. I had begged her for so long to get me on a team. I even scoured the street on trash pickup day for months to collect cans and bottles so that I could contribute money for the fees. Given our financial circumstances, my mom wanted to give me whatever she could, like any parent would. There was so much we couldn't have. But she also knew how dangerous the game could be. The film *Concussion* hadn't yet been made, and CTE (chronic traumatic encephalopathy) hadn't yet been covered in the news, but any reasonable person who had ever seen a football game could see the risk. She told me she thought it was dangerous, and I could see she was concerned. She didn't want her baby to get hurt. But I could also tell from the way she said it that she was on the fence.

Football, like so many things in life, comes down to a basic risk-versus-reward equation. In neighborhoods like mine, that equation is a lot different from how it is in other places. A passionate player with some talent and potential has many reasons not to dwell on the dangers of the game. Sadly, sports like football could mean so much for a kid's future. And it had a lot of impact even on day-to-day life as a young man in an underserved inner-city neighborhood. So if and when a player saw a serious injury on the field, he'd put it out of his head and get on to the next play.

Like anybody in my community, my mom knew what football could mean to a young black man. Where I'm from, sports and entertainment are presented to us as the only option to feed our future families. The game could get me into a high-quality private high school, and a scholarship could be my golden ticket into college. And then there was the lottery the NFL Draft represented. Even a modest NFL contract could set us all up for life. Not too many people in the hood see pursuing education as an end in and of itself or even as a means to a better life, even though the likelihood of success in becoming a doctor or lawyer is much greater than in becoming an NFL player. I would later work to help people in my community understand this and change their mind-set.

My mom also knew that football would keep me away from the negative influences and dangers in school and on the street. Busy days mean kids have fewer chances to cross paths with the violence and crime that is so much a part of impoverished inner-city neighborhoods. Idle time is the Devil's playground.

Despite all that, I realized I was going to have to push her a little bit. With the help of Coach Tony, that's exactly what I did. He had told my mom, "Look, if you don't want the boy to play football, I'll respect that. You have to do what's right for him. But at least come out to a practice and take a look. Maybe you'll change your mind."

I could tell he was setting it up for me. When she told me she'd take me to a practice, I said, "Mom, if we're going to go watch the practice, the least I could do is have on the proper shoes. In case I want to run around a little, I don't want to be slipping all over the place."

Of course she knew perfectly well what I was up to, but I think she was between a rock and hard place. On the weekend, she took me to Kmart and we bought the cheapest cleats they had—a pair of rubber Rawlings baseball cleats. They were maybe the most horrible things you could wear for football, like strapping your feet to wood blocks with spikes. But I had cleats. I wore them home from the store. The next day at church I wore the cleats with my jeans. I didn't think twice about the possibility that the cleats would start to wear down. It was more about the opportunity that they represented for me. I might be able to play football now.

The day of the practice, my mom and I jumped in the car to drive to the field. On the way, she dropped a bomb.

"Oh, by the way, this is Snoop Dogg's league."

I was like, "Snoop Dogg? As in Snoop Doggy Dog. Snoopy D. O. Double G?"

"Yeah."

"Will we meet him?"

"I'm sure we will, sooner or later."

I said to myself, *Wow, I could get to play football for Snoop Dogg?* The world had suddenly gotten a lot brighter. Snoop Dogg was a legend in the hood. Not just because he was a platinum-selling rapper from the streets but also because he was giving back in a major way. He knew better than anyone how young black men were struggling in the downtrodden neighborhoods of

Southern California. And he was doing everything he could to help them.

The music I had been exposed to in Fontana was reggae, because my father loved Jamaican culture, but I stopped listening to it after we left. Rap, on the other hand, is the pulse of the inner city. Miss Pam, the woman who took care of us in the afternoons when we first started attending our new school, would keep the BET channel on almost all day. She would watch endless rap videos, and the music spoke to me about exactly what I was going through.

It's easy to dismiss rap music and the messages that much of it contains, because rap is the story of a culture, coded and delivered for a specific audience. For young black kids trying to make sense of the problems in their families and the harsh realities they face every day, rap illuminates their experiences, puts things in context. I hate how the music often focuses on drugs, violence, and the degradation of women, but those are the realities of Compton, Newark, Watts, and Chicago. Snoop, for example, spoke the raw truth of life in poverty in the hood and on the streets. Some of it was hard to hear, but it was real. He rapped about life under the thumb of the system—the police, the courts, and social services—and traumatized parents. Songs like Snoop's are often criticized for condoning drugs, crime, and violence, but they are speaking truth to the power of the limited options young black males face in the dark corners of America. There are lots of levels to those songs. At least in the golden era of rap, with N.W.A., Tupac, Nas, Notorious B.I.G., and Public Enemy, the songs were a way for people in terrible situations to grapple with their conditions and assert some control.

For those who don't like rap music, that's fine. But my hope is that they have an equal or even greater disdain for, along with a passion to change, the systems and circumstances that create the content in rap.

So even though my mom played gospel at home, I became a rap fan early on. Although most of the rap I heard was the censored version, by sixth grade I was regularly listening to Eminem, 50 Cent, and other rappers. My favorite, though, was Nas, one of the most positive artists. He put out a song that was my anthem, called "I Can." The song encourages youth from the ghetto to stay focused and know their worth. It was aspirational and empowering, promoting the idea that whatever you want to achieve is within your grasp if you're willing to sacrifice and work hard for it. He referenced black men and women as descended from kings and queens, and pushed the idea of respecting yourself. That message meant so much to me coming from an icon like Nas. So, the idea that I might meet a legendary rapper and play football? That seemed like winning the lottery to me.

Coach Tony was a man of character, a man of God,

but he knew how to be persuasive. We parked the car at the park where the Falcons practiced and walked up to where he was standing with his whistle around his neck and his clipboard in hand. He smiled and greeted my mother warmly. He was good natured and kind, in a place where good-natured and kind people can be a rare commodity. As he started the first drill, he casually leaned over toward my mom and me and said in a low voice, "Don't you want him to join in, at least have a little fun?" Then he spiked the shot, saying to me, "Or you just want to watch?"

No, I did not just want to watch.

Pity my mom. She was in the worst position possible. She obviously had real reservations about me being on that field. And she knew that once I stepped onto it, she was never going to get me off it. The train would leave the station and she wouldn't have another chance to stop it. On the other hand, all three of us standing there knew that if she said no, the other parents clustered around us would judge her as an overprotective mother raising a mama's boy. It would be a slam on both of us, especially in our neighborhood where respect counted for so much. It's not like Coach Tony couldn't do that math. I loved Coach Tony for that.

All she could do was nod. He smiled and said to me, "Come on. Hop on out into the drill." I was the last kid to leave the field that day, and by the time I went to bed, my mom had given up and said I could join the Falcons. We had gone through so much, and her kids had seen so many things kids shouldn't see, she knew a gift she could give when she saw it.

But in reality, neither my mom nor I knew what I was actually getting into by joining the Falcons. At that time there were five levels in the Snoop Dogg league. In ascending order, they are: Junior Clinic, Clinic, Junior Pee Wee, Pee Wee, and Junior Midget. The Falcons team Coach Tony ran was a Pee Wee team, a team for twelve- and thirteen-year-olds. I was ten. That is a big three-year gap in the physical maturity of a young man. The other kids on the team were all noticeably larger, stronger, and faster. Some had light facial hair sprouting on their faces. I was often the quickest kid in street games with my neighbors and at school. But compared to these kids? I was nowhere near fast.

It was a rough season, but that first year with the Falcons helped make me a really tough player. I wasn't very good, but it honed my tenacity. I prided myself in being a tough tackler, twice taking down future University of Oregon and NFL star player De'Anthony Thomas, who played for the Crenshaw Bears. I loved the game and wanted to be better, so I worked harder than I might have in a lower-level team. All I really had was my aggressiveness. I could hit hard and I was never going to quit.

The equivalent to Little League right field on a youth

football team is wide receiver or cornerback, because passing isn't really part of the game with young kids. So those were my positions on the Falcons, even though I'd always wanted to play quarterback like I did in my neighborhood games. That first year, I didn't get to touch the football much, but the upside was that I worked on the tackling and hitting skills that would serve me for the rest of my football career. I developed devastating hitting abilities because that's about all I ever did of worth during games.

Adding football to schoolwork and commuting made for busy days. The Falcons practiced Monday through Friday from six to eight at night. Games were held on Saturdays at three in the afternoon. Dodson Middle School was about a fifteen-mile bus ride from where I lived. After twelve hours of school, bus travel, and homework, I'd hop in my mom's car and head to practice.

The danger of football games is actually multiplied in practice. There are even more opportunities for injury there than in game play. Some of the drills actually seem designed to injure. The graveyard drill is an example. It's a common one-on-one practice drill that I went through dozens of times. One player is on offense, one on defense. They lay down on their backs with their heads pointed at each other. One has a ball and one doesn't. The coaches lay down a narrow lane defined by cones so that you cannot avoid contact. When the coach blows the whistle, both players jump to their feet and then run full speed at each other. The offensive player tries to get "through" the defensive player; the guy on defense is trying to bring down the offensive player. More often than not, the collisions are helmet to helmet. It's where I first had my bell rung.

But the danger isn't limited to helmet-to-helmet contact. That's just the part of the game that gets the most attention. Sure, full-speed helmet-to-helmet hits can cause concussions and injuries. But your brain is basically free-floating inside your skull. It's protected all around by a layer of fluid. If your skull is moving quickly in one direction and comes to a sudden halt, the brain keeps moving until it contacts the inside of the skull. That can happen when a player hits another player in the head, but it can also occur when a player is tackled and his head whiplashes to the ground. It can happen in lots of ways. People get concussions falling down in their homes or in low-speed car accidents.

And that's not even considering cut blocks that can bend knees in ways they're not supposed to bend, or what happens when your cleat gets stuck and your foot doesn't turn with the rest of your leg. Football players even risk a broken wrist when they do the natural thing and put out a hand to break a hard fall. It's a tough, physical game.

That first year, before I learned how to properly minimize contact—to make and take hits—I was constantly being battered. The connection didn't dawn on me at the time, but I had headaches every day during the sixth-grade football season. Sometimes they were blinding, so painful I'd lay in the dark until they faded. Sometimes I would havc to miss a day or two of school. I just thought that every kid had headaches. But to be honest, even if I had known that football was causing them, I would have just kept on playing. That is the raw truth behind all inner-city football. Quitting really isn't an option because there's nothing else to replace it. Give up football and you walk away a coward, at least in the eyes of everyone around you. Now I have different thoughts about leaving the game.

My second year on the Falcons was much more satisfying. The headaches went away in the off-season and would never return. It was a matter of learning how to play properly. You can minimize the danger inherent in the sport by using basic techniques like staying low and keeping your feet in motion so that the energy of a hit is dissipated. You learn to "wrap up" as you tackle rather than lead with your head. Instead of using your head, you rely more on your shoulders and leg power. Your body gets more tuned to responding to on-field situations and reacting to limit any possible injury. It shouldn't be surprising how many injuries happen in football at every level; the really amazing thing is the many injuries that don't occur.

That second football season got off to a memorable

start. After the Falcons wrapped up summer training, the league had its annual end-of-summer block party, where I finally got to meet Snoop Dogg. The party was held in Country Crossing Park in Pomona. The event is called Family Fun Day, and Snoop is adamant about limiting adults. He doesn't want people pitching him business ideas, or any weird stuff. It's a day for the youth, with no gang members or police in sight. For a whole day we could run around and just be kids in a safe environment, a few hundred of us. We filled our bellies to bursting with hot dogs, cheeseburgers, soda, and snow cones. For most of us, it was more food than we could imagine. There was a bouncy house, water balloons, and fun from one end of the park to the other. Parents stood around in team T-shirts, watching, talking to each other, but staying out of the kids' way.

When my turn came to meet Snoop, I could hardly believe it. He was impossibly tall and grandiose in stature, but approachable at the same time. He was wearing his wraparound shades and Pomona Steelers T-shirt (his local team), and I smiled like my face was going to split. I said, "What up, Coach Snoop?"

He smiled back and said, "What up, nephew?" Years later, we would connect again, but right at that moment, he was just the man who made it all happen.

My second year in the league was a chance to grow, to expand my skills and define who I was going to be on the field. My quickness was now more on par with all the other kids on the field, and I took over my chosen position as quarterback. I became the starter during the summer before our first game. I loved playing quarterback because I had so much control and it was such a challenge. I had to keep my head about me, see the field in three dimensions, and know where everyone was. But I also played defense because most players in youth football play both ways. I would play defensive end or linebacker, and it would give me a chance to let out my aggression. I tried to be on the field as much as I could, playing on special teams and returning kicks as well.

The Falcons practiced in Harvard Park in South Central, right in the middle of gang territory. The truth is, there is a complex relationship between street gangs and football. Gang leaders aren't stupid; they know that football teams take prospective gang members off the street and onto the field. But there is a great deal of respect for football and football players in neighborhoods like Compton, Watts, and South Central. There's a tradition of it. Gangs don't get in the middle of football leagues, but the leagues do have to tread carefully and be street smart about what they're doing. The real dangers of inner-city football aren't limited to the playing field.

The league president, Keith Johnson, who also coached one of the teams, had a relationship with gang leaders. The Falcons had two liaison police officers assigned to the league who alerted the coaches to gang activity. Often gang leaders themselves would let us know when we shouldn't be in the park. A member of the Bloods might show up at practice and say, "Hey, we just want to let y'all know there's going to be a lot of red up here later, so you probably want to be clear by then." Or the police officers assigned to the team would tell us that we had to find somewhere else to practice because they had intel that there might be retaliation for some earlier fight. There could be shots.

The Southern California Falcons' colors are red and black, a canny choice on the part of the league. Harvard Park and the field where we played our games were both Six Deuce Brims territory. The Six Deuce Brims is one of the oldest, largest, and most violent Blood gangs in America. They represent themselves with red bandannas and shirts. So parents wearing Falcon team gear in the parking lot outside a youth football game would never be in danger of repping another gang. Nor would the players. It removed the possibility of a potentially fatal mistake in identity. Had the team played in Crips territory—the Bloods' rival, represented by the color blue—someone could have been shot simply for wearing a big red Falcons team T-shirt in support of her son.

In Compton and places like it, what you wear can be a matter of life and death. Some rough-looking dude walks up to you at the bus stop and says, "Where you from?" But he's not asking where you live or where you were born. He's seen your football practice jersey and he's asking if you're affiliated with a gang from another area. He's asking if you and him are going to have a problem. He might be asking if he's going to have to shoot you on principle. I'd say, "Nah, man, these aren't my colors. I just play football for the Falcons in the Snoop League."

"Oh, that's wassup. I got a cousin who plays for the Compton Vikings." He'd let it go.

My favorite color became gray.

The story that fashion told included my experience at Dodson, where students who lived locally would have the latest sneakers and most popular player jerseys, setting them apart from those of us who made the trip to the school from outside the area. I sometimes wore the same clothes three days in a row. I would just rotate my three differently colored pairs of socks so no one would catch on.

But I didn't worry about the clothes. I was safe at Dodson. More than that, it provided a superior education. The classes were exceptional because the teachers were exceptional. The money and resources available were phenomenal. I remember being amazed that the PE class had a Dance Dance Revolution arcade game for students to use and RipStik skateboards to hone their balance on. All the books were new or close to it, and the library was large and well appointed. Unlike schools closer to my house, if you found a book in the Dodson library catalog, you could be sure it would be on the shelf. I was attracted to Dodson because somewhere deep down I understood that as crucial as football was to my path out of the hood, education was going to be even more critical. Just as the Southern California Falcons were teaching me basic skills I could build on as I progressed in my football career, Dodson, with its high standards and dedicated staff, was laying a foundation that I could stand on to step up in my education.

The move beyond Dodson, to high school, would involve the intersection of the three main forces in my life: football, academics, and faith. All that would take place in a shining beacon founded by Jesuits in the wake of the famous Watts riots, and that beacon would take me into the belly of the inner-city beast, a neighborhood even worse than Compton.

4

QUESTION: *"What will you do to change the narrative and legacy in your community?"*

A place like Verbum Dei seemed beyond my grasp in sixth grade. I had initially struggled at Dodson Middle School. My entire sixth-grade year was an academic disaster because I was living in fear. The public bus ride to Dodson was a frightening experience. I faced real threats and took real risks every day. I saw my backpack as an inconvenience because it would weigh me down if I needed to run or to fight. Eventually I just left it at home. That meant I wasn't able to bring schoolwork and class notes home or take homework back to my classes at Dodson. By midway through the school year I was barely scratching out Cs and Ds. Finally, my English and history teacher, a kindly older woman named Mrs. Walters, sat me down and told it to me plain.

"You're not a gang member."

"What?" I was startled, looking into those unblinking deep-green eyes.

"You're not a gang member. I see great things in you, and I see a great student in you. But it will require that you bring your backpack to school every day."

That she would single me out and take the time and concern to honestly say what needed to be said left a mark. I took her words to heart. I started to bring my backpack to school again. Mrs. Walters reawakened in me the understanding that I needed to get back on my homework assignments if I wanted to succeed in life. I made sure I always caught the early bus at 6:04 a.m. to avoid any trouble that would lead me to drop my backpack and take off running. I would occasionally ditch my sixth-period physical education class ten minutes early to run down the hill to the bus stop and catch the 3:15 p.m. bus. PE was my favorite class. It allowed me to release all my youthful masculine energy and aggression. I hated that I had to ditch the class, but that few minutes ensured I would have a smooth ride home and could continue to carry my homework-filled backpack.

Dodson was an opportunity, one that I had fought to get. I realized it would be foolish to waste it, and no way was I going to be a fool. I stepped up. In seventh grade I maintained a 4.0 grade point average and did almost that well in eighth grade. The fall of my eighth-grade year, I was playing under a new coach in the Junior Midget division, the highest level in the Snoop Youth Football League. Like all the league's coaches, Coach Glover took it upon himself to not only coach but to mentor his players as well. He wanted to know what was going on in each player's life and that they were taking care of business off the field. One day after practice he asked me about my high school plans.

"Where do you think you want to go?"

"I wanna go to Serra. That's where I'm applying."

He made a face. "Man, don't go there. Go to Verbum Dei."

"What's that?"

"That's the school I'm sending my son to right now. It's like a little college campus. You get there, you have to wear a shirt and tie. You have to be professional, and it's a guarantee that you'll go to college." He was so nonchalant but firm at the same time that I took notice.

But Junipero Serra High School in Gardena was an alluring football powerhouse. Every year, several Serra graduates went on to Division I football programs and were then drafted into the NFL. The education was better than local public schools and, just as important, it was a Christian school. That was crucial to both my mom and me. My faith sustained me through tough times when no person could or would. Sometimes, in the worst moments, I felt like God was the only one who saw or heard me.

My mom called the Junipero Serra admissions office to discuss getting me in. But they were dismissive and rude to her. They seemed put off by the many questions she asked them about the curriculum, opportunities where character and leadership would be developed, community service, and college counseling and support. I'm not sure if the admissions person was being elitist or if they had never met a person like my mom. One thing that I am sure of is that they didn't understand what my mom was interested in doing: taking a young black boy into manhood. I mentioned to my mom what Coach Glover had said about Verbum Dei. It, too, was a religious high school and proudly boasted that 100 percent of their graduates went on to college. My mom set up a campus tour.

The Verbum Dei campus sits right in the middle of what looks like an urban war zone. The school was founded in 1962 but became vital to the community in the aftermath of the Watts riots in 1965. The riots left most of Watts in ruins to one degree or another, and the neighborhood remains incredibly destitute and dangerous. As bad as Compton might have been, Watts was worse. It was the hood of the hood. Verbum Dei High School was a diamond in the middle of inconceivable blight. Founded by Jesuits, the school's name is Latin for "Word of God." However, unlike many other private religious high schools in Los Angeles, Verbum Dei isn't an elitist institution. The all-male school has a unique model. Every student participates in a work-study program that not only gives the student valuable professional experience and contacts but also pays for the student's tuition.

Verbum Dei tasks itself with building mentally strong young men. The mission is for every graduate to be open to personal growth; be intellectually motivated, spiritual, loving, and committed to justice; and to be experienced with the professional work environment.

The school I would come to know as "Verb" is not visually impressive. It has simple, squared-off institutional buildings and clean, basic athletic facilities. The most impressive thing on campus is the student body. As I walked around the grounds in late spring, all the students looked sharp with short haircuts, black slacks, white button-down shirts, and ties. I noticed one senior in particular, a Latino with the name *Jovel* stitched on the back of his letterman's jacket. He had some swag, greeting everybody he passed with a broad, genuine smile and a few words of familiar greeting. He appeared to be totally comfortable in his own skin and beamed with confidence. When one of the teachers stopped him, they engaged in a somber discussion. You could see the adult took him seriously and the student communicated to the teacher with respect and deference. I wanted to be that guy. I wanted to be surrounded by people who shared my drive and hope for the future. By the time we got back to the car for the ten-minute drive home down Central Avenue, I knew I had found my academic home.

I filled out the Verbum Dei application form that night. On Monday, I asked my eighth-grade dean, Rachel Whitlow, for a letter of recommendation. She wrote kind words about my work ethic, devotion to my studies, and sociability. All I needed to do was ace the interview.

Verbum Dei interviews are conducted by a three-person panel. The head of the committee was a stern, serious man named Mr. Willis. He was tall and exuded strength of presence. He had a somber look on his face, and he styled his hair in a short, no-nonsense cut. He wore a gray business suit, the finest I had ever seen in person. The committee members proceeded to ask profound, thoughtful questions. I sat there in a stiff wooden chair, fielding question after question.

"What is it to be a 'real man'?"

"Where do you see yourself after leaving Verbum Dei?"

"How do you see yourself contributing to this campus?"

"Define the word 'character.'"

These were important questions I had thought about many times, even as a thirteen-year-old. This was what Verbum Dei was all about. The school was bringing order to chaotic young lives. They were providing purpose and direction to those who needed it most. I already shared the school's values—faith in God, love of education, personal discipline. All I had to do was show them that I could be a true Verbum Dei gentleman—a young man of faith, character, and integrity. When I received the acceptance letter in the mail, I wasn't surprised. The school was a perfect fit. But I was incredibly happy and grateful. Verbum Dei was the next step on my personal path out of the hood to whatever lay beyond.

I began my Verbum Dei career with summer two-a-day football practices. They couldn't have been more different from the Falcons' workouts. Youth football focuses on contact—tackling or avoiding being tackled. The emphasis is on the basics. Building blocks. Plays are kept simple: a "thirty-two dive" meant the three-back takes the ball and runs through the two hole. Or you might do a very basic sweep-right play. Maybe an option play around the outside. Verb's playbook and practices were more technical and nuanced. There was suddenly an emphasis on proper footwork. The quarterback regularly used a five-step drop, which hinges on proper foot placement, quickness, and timing. We had screen plays, which required coordination and perfect timing. I learned to read defensive coverages, check down possible receivers, anticipate routes, and throw passes before a receiver even turned his head. I started to see the complexity in the game, how you could visualize defensive positions and weaknesses as a quarterback. Because opposing teams would steal signals, getting the plays from the sidelines was a case of sifting through false hand signals thrown up by different coaches to determine the play to run. At all times, you had to pay attention and think, not just look to hit the open guy or hand off the ball. I loved the challenge. I loved all of it. It raised my game.

The Verbum Dei Eagles were not the athletic powerhouse that the Junipero Serra Cavaliers were, but we made the playoffs every year I was there, and we won the league championship in my sophomore year. We might have been even more successful had the players not been subjected to unusual academic rigor. Any Verb player who didn't maintain a 2.5 grade point average would not be allowed to play. Because the first grades came out halfway through our season, inevitably we would lose a good number of key players at that point. At other schools, they might be saved by the fact that the coach was also their history or math teacher and would let them slide. Or other teachers could be convinced to bump grades a notch, to help out important players in the name of school spirit and supporting the team. They didn't do it like that at Verb. Education and character came first.

Academics were far from the only challenge players faced. Though littered with gopher holes, the school's football field was well maintained and wasn't in danger of being co-opted by the Bloods like the Falcons' field, but Verbum Dei's campus faced issues similar to those of other inner-city schools. The campus faces out onto the wide lanes of the infamous South Central Avenue, where any kid in a Verbum Dei blazer was a potential target for robbery or assault. Homeless drug addicts and drunks clustered in groups and makeshift shelters along the train tracks on one side of the school. Drug syringes and crack pipes were scattered among the rubbish along the tracks. The football field was a buffer between the actual school buildings and the largest housing project west of the Mississippi River, Nickerson Gardens, which lined the back fence and threw an ominous shadow over the field.

The field was—unlike the Falcons' practice fields—private property, but that didn't stop the locals. Some people in the projects resented the school, and football practice was an easy opportunity to show it. We would be scrimmaging when suddenly a volley of rocks would come flying over the fence, a message from the disenfranchised and frustrated youths on the other side. They yelled insults and abuse on a regular basis. And when they got no reaction to their taunts, and there were enough of them to muster a mob mentality and false courage, they might jump the fence and start fights with the players. The part that they forgot was that the players on the field were from similar backgrounds; we had no problem handling ourselves in a fistfight.

This is the kind of senselessness that systemic oppression and hopelessness breed. It is a peculiar syndrome familiar to anyone who has lived in an underserved community: people become so hyperaware of who has something, and who doesn't, that they strike out at their own when they sense someone—on the block, in the neighborhood, at the trailer park, on the other side of that fence—has an advantage. It's a predictable expression of constantly suppressed frustration and rage, even though it's grossly misplaced. Those Nickerson Garden residents didn't really know who they were mad at; they were just mad. And I couldn't blame them; I often felt that same anger. All they knew is that they were born in a project building where there were spikes on the fences that turn inward to keep people in. Then you see a group of well-dressed kids on the other side of the fence, trying to rise above everything? I knew that we had a responsibility not only to the school but to Watts, to be lights that shined there, illumination for those who might never otherwise see the light.

The school itself was a sanctuary for the students in many ways. Most students would commute in by car or city bus, hustling in each morning under the cover of the entryway, with its roof shaped like a stuck-out tongue. We would either bring our lunches in plastic grocery bags or—for those of us who could afford it—eat in the cafeteria. Due to a history of robberies and violence, we weren't allowed to grab a bite to eat on South Central Avenue during lunch breaks. You could easily get caught "slippin'" and make a turn down a street that could compromise your health.

One day every week was dedicated to the Corporate Work Study Program, which was basically an internship. Shuttles would take us to high-rise office buildings in downtown Los Angeles or other enclaves full of nondescript corporate parks. I worked at a property management company in Pasadena, called Shea Properties, until the summer before my senior year. That last year,

I interned at Union Bank in the business systems analyst department. I got the chance to work with data sets and to become familiar with how databases are organized and analyzed. The work experience was a perfect complement to my classroom work. During my lunch breaks I walked around and explored downtown Los Angeles. I would eventually wander over by the public library to eat at one of my favorite fast-food spots, Panda Express. I usually had fried rice, kung pao chicken, and sweetfire chicken. I enjoyed eating there because it gave me an opportunity to talk to the homeless people outside the library and hear their stories. Working at Union Bank also gave me the opportunity to meet Carl Ballton, the president of the Union Bank Foundation. He became a valuable mentor. I would regularly meet and talk with him, and he would buy me lunch. I would sit across from him, slowly finishing my fries, while he counseled me about college and life.

"You know who W. E. B. DuBois was?"

"A writer and scholar."

"A *black* writer and scholar. A thinker. DuBois told us that African Americans will never matriculate in an upward manner until we have a thorough understanding of economics. You get it?"

"Major in economics?"

"Major in economics, right. That's where you start. That's where it all starts."

There were many sources of guidance and inspiration

in that world. Classes at Verbum Dei were rigorous. There was no place to hide because classes were rarely larger than ten people. This wasn't a typical hood school; there were no teachers just doing time, trying to keep the class quiet and calm. Many of my teachers had "Doctor" before their names. Teachers at Verb were accomplished and demanding, pushing us to find the best within ourselves. The pace discouraged bad study habits. Homework wasn't optional, and it got done one way or another. If you made excuses and didn't get it done at home, or if it was done poorly as a rushed afterthought, you would get JUG. An abbreviation for the Latin term meaning "burden," the students commonly but understandably mistook it to mean "Justice Under God." There are many versions of the punishment, but at Verb it meant losing your lunch period and sitting in silent contemplation of your actions. If you brought food, you could eat, but usually you wouldn't. Verbum Dei also has a classic demerit system, but I was careful to avoid demerits. I knew that if I broke the rules, I risked losing my privilege to play football.

The only infraction I ever got busted for was using the weight room off hours. The school limited weight-room time and a coach had to be present, but I stuck tape on the latch and would go in and work out after school, even when we had a dance or other school event. I got caught more than once trying to get big and strong. The athletic director didn't punish me because it wasn't like some of the other infractions, such as smoking. But he sure would yell at me. As he scolded me for "always disobeying the school weight-room policy," I would hold in my laugh. I would say to myself, *If this dude thinks that I'm going to put my dreams on hold for some dumb rule, then he has me confused with someone else. This is all I got.* I kept the tape on me at all times. I would be back the next day.

The dress code was as rigorous as any of the other rules. A button-down shirt, black tie, dark dress pants, and black dress shoes were all required. And all of it had to be clean and pressed. Given that many students were struggling through life in Watts, and the rest of us lived in places like Compton, Crenshaw, and Inglewood, keeping your uniform squared away could be a challenge. But it was part of the discipline of Verbum Dei, and I took to it. Every day at Verb felt like a step away from the hood and one yard closer to the goal line, toward success.

My sister and brother were having much different educational experiences. Mi had been accepted into one of the most exclusive prep schools in Los Angeles: Harbor Teacher Preparation Academy in Wilmington. The school offered a curriculum where students could earn an associate's degree at the same time they got their high school diploma. However, in her first year, Mi had been overwhelmed by the academic load and rigor. She had fallen behind in her classes and done poorly. Only much later would my mom and school officials figure out that this could have been avoided had Mi been given the care and attention needed for her impediments to learning, but by then she had transferred to our local high school. Mi had to spend time avoiding gang members, trying to learn in classes with forty students and a rotating seating schedule because there weren't enough chairs for everyone, and dealing with striking teachers who were outraged that there were not enough textbooks for their classes. Mi would ultimately use those difficulties as a springboard for her academic comeback.

Chase was struggling as well. I had been luckier than Chase. I had come into elementary school with a strong foundation from almost two years at Sugar Hill Elementary in Moreno Valley, and competing in the spelling bee in second grade had netted me a spot in the magnet program. I could read, and I understood how to discipline myself and how to tackle homework. Chase went into our new school not knowing how to read and made it through to the end of first grade still illiterate. Kids don't fall through the cracks at a place like this; the entire school is a crack. Just another crevice in an incredibly damaged—and damaging—system. My brother's situation was certainly shocking, but far from unusual.

As a result, he couldn't meet the entrance standards for Dodson or any other local advanced school. He wound up at the middle school I had fought so hard to avoid. While I was laying the groundwork for college with challenging honors classes and the high expectations of teachers and school officials, Chase was doing all he could not to be a statistic, another black face from the hood getting crushed by a system and culture that looks at black students as irritations at best and often considers them totally disposable.

During his time there, Chase got involved with gangs, ditching class, and smoking weed. He slowly started to become a product of his environment. At one point he told me that he was jealous of a friend, Ralphie, who brought his older brother's loaded 45-magnum to school. Chase wanted his own piece, which alarmed me. Chase was a follower. It was a bad situation that I realized was quickly becoming much worse. I decided to intervene.

One day my mom got a call from school about Chase. He had been standing on his desk and jumping off of it like a superhero. He brought a Batman cape to school and was going around calling himself "Crack Man." He was acting a fool to impress all his buddies in class. The girls also took a stronger liking to you when you rebelled against authority in school. My mom had to take time off of work to go in and meet with the principal and youth counselors at the school. I told her I wanted to go with her. She understood why.

My mom had already told Chase he couldn't play football because of his bad grades. But there in the counselor's office, as three school officials looked on, she spoke truth to him in no uncertain terms. She told him that he wasn't so old that she couldn't spank him right there in that office, and that he should start thinking about the repercussions of his actions and what came next. After about twenty minutes of her doing all the talking, I walked Chase back to his classroom. As we turned down a hallway, I looked behind me to see if anyone was there. Then I open-hand slapped that boy right on the back of his head. I didn't believe in violence then, and I still don't now. But on that day, as a fourteen-year-old, I wasn't mature enough to find any other way to communicate my message: you will *not* be dead or in jail by age eighteen.

Then, right there in the classroom in front of his little buddies, I had my say.

"Is this who you're trying to impress? These clowns? You think you're all bad? You aren't nothing. You want to be successful? Or you want to be like them, the rest of your life in the hood, being nobody? Is that what you want?"

Chase didn't say anything, because there was nothing he could say. He just looked embarrassed, like he wanted to sink into the floor and disappear. But there was worse waiting for him when he got home. I had piled his clothes and the rest of his stuff in the hall outside our bedroom. He was shocked. "Why you put my stuff in the hallway?"

"Listen, you walk into this room anytime I'm in here, I'm beating you up. When I eat, if I'm at the high table, you eat at the lower table. If I'm at the lower table, you sit cross-legged on the ground. You don't deserve to sit where I eat, and you don't deserve to sleep where I sleep."

He looked like he was about to cry as the reality of what I was saying sunk in. It wasn't just that he was going to be humbled anytime he was in that house but also that he had lost the respect of his family who had been so supportive of him. He knew he had a lot of ground to make up.

I told him, "I'm putting in the work every single day to make the most out of life, and to make something out of nothing, for the future. Not just for me, but for my community and my family. You literally working in the opposite direction of where I'm trying to go. You didn't earn this bed, you didn't earn this food. I earned this bed and this food. I should take your food away from you, but you need to eat so you can study."

True to my word, Chase slept in the hall for a month—until he pulled up his grades and we got a good report from his school that he wasn't causing any problems in class. It would take him a while to completely get his act together. He'd squeak by to graduation but would really dedicate himself with a vigorous work ethic to follow in my footsteps years later. He would attend Verbum Dei, where he would ultimately make the honor roll every semester he was there.

Life at Verb might have been tough, but it wasn't like the other high schools in Watts. It wasn't Jordan High

School or Locke High School tough. There was no metal-detector cop checking backpacks. It didn't grind you down; it built you up. The challenges were predictable. They expected a lot from me, but I expected a lot from myself. Many of the temptations, however, were the same: peer pressure to fit in, to gangbang, to drink, to smoke. I never had a problem with those temptations, because to me, they led right back to the hood. I knew from a young age that if I partied, lived the lifestyle that other guys bragged about in the locker room, I could get stuck in the hood. That wasn't an option.

If I needed a reminder of all that was at stake, I got it one August afternoon before the start of my sophomore year.

Thursday, August 27, 2009, was partly cloudy and hot. I was on the football field at Verb, at an afternoon preseason practice. My mom, brother, and sister were at home. It was a relaxing afternoon for them before the start of the school year, and they had just settled in to watch a movie. They hadn't even got through the credits when the house began to shake. A police helicopter was hovering so low that it was vibrating the entire structure.

Police helicopters were a common, sometimes daily, occurrence in our neighborhood. It was how the police tracked somebody trying to elude them in a car or on foot. That distinctive *whoop-whoop-whoop* was as much a soundtrack of my youth as rap was. It was a sound you felt as much as heard. But they didn't usually get low enough to cause a house to shake. My mom realized they were hovering right over the house. Then she heard a voice over a loudspeaker say our address and command: "Residents. Come out slowly with your hands in the air."

Everyone went to the front picture window and looked out. The street was lined with black-and-white LAPD police cars, their Christmas-tree lights flashing. Cops surrounded the property, pointing shotguns at the house.

"Residents, come out now!"

With the TV still playing, my mom led my brother and sister to the front door and slowly opened it. She held her breath, hoping that neither she nor her kids would be shot. They walked outside, one after the other, with their hands held as high as they could hold them.

The cops put everyone in separate police cruisers while officers began to search the house. Then they questioned my mom, brother, and sister. They asked them if my father had attempted to contact any of them. Obviously my father was in serious trouble, but the police didn't give my mom any details. After an hour or so, they left.

Back inside the house, my mom checked the local news channels and saw a report that my father had allegedly shot someone and that he was the subject of a citywide manhunt. There was little chance that he knew where I went to school, but she decided not to risk it. She put Chase and Mi in the car and drove to Verbum Dei.

We were practicing in light gear—jersey, shorts, helmet, and cleats—without tackling. I was about to run a play when a coach ran onto the field from the sideline.

"Caylin, you need to go with your mom."

My mom was standing on the sidelines with two other coaches. There was a police car filled with cops idling next to my mom's car. I jogged over to her, wondering what the heck was going on.

"We've got to go, baby. I'll tell you why in the car."

I changed out of my cleats, left my helmet in my locker, and met my mom in the parking lot. Chase and Mi were in the car, looking worried and stressed out. Sitting in the parking lot, my mom told me what had happened at the house and what she knew from the news report.

"The police are looking for your father. They say he killed someone. I don't know what he's doing, but we need to stay together until they find him."

It shook me up. It was obvious to me that my mom thought my dad was a danger to us. I couldn't imagine that he would try to hurt us, but then again, I couldn't imagine him killing someone either. It crushed a part of me. It had been hard enough not having my father in my life while I was growing up, but to have him do something so bad, so vicious? This was my blood they were talking about. It kind of made me feel as though I was partly responsible. I was ashamed. That was as far down as you could get. My head was spinning, but my mom was determined that we would keep things as normal as possible.

From my days in the Snoop League, my mom had become increasingly involved in youth football, eventually training as a coach. She had become the head coach of the Clinic Falcons team in the Valley Youth Football League in San Fernando Valley. I volunteered as her assistant coach and would normally go to her team practice after the Verbum Dei afternoon practice. So, rather than take us back home where my brother and sister had just been traumatized, my mom decided to follow our routine and go to her team practice. When we got there, she spoke with the other coaches at length, letting them know what was going on and asking that they be aware of anything out of the ordinary. Then she got on with practice.

I went through the motions of directing player drills. But I was numb. It all seemed unbelievable. Chase helped me run the drills. Mi was a cheer coach, so she worked with the cheerleaders. Time passed in a fog. Finally practice wrapped up and we drove home. Walking into the house, I felt drained. I started a book on the Verbum Dei reading list that had been sent out in anticipation of the new school year. I found myself going over and over the same paragraph, not really reading, not really focusing. Eventually I just gave up and went to bed to the sound of *Samurai Jack* cartoons on the TV.

Around ten that night, the police called my mom.

They had arrested my father, whom they had found walking down the street in Riverside in a drunken stupor. We would eventually piece together what had happened from the police reports, news articles, and court transcripts. Early that morning my father had been holed up in his apartment in Fontana, where he lived with his girlfriend, Jillian White. He was forty-five; she was a twenty-seven-year-old white woman.

Apparently, my father owed some bad people money, and they had made it clear to him that they were going get paid or make an example of him. He hid out in his apartment, drinking, smoking pot, and passing time. He and Jillian had been hanging around the apartment all day long, getting high and drunk, and arguing about trivial things. He had a rifle. When she went out, she came back to find the door locked and began pounding on it, eventually finding her keys and opening the door. Drunk, high, and confused, he thought it was the people who were after him breaking into the apartment. He shot her once in the shoulder as she walked through the door. Then he shot her twice in the back as she spun around. Realizing what he had done, he fled. The police, while looking for him, showed up at my grandmother's house.

The next year and a half would unravel what little was left of my father's life. I would follow the different court hearings and the trial itself at a distance. In the end, my father was convicted and sentenced to fifty-two years to life. I couldn't motivate myself to care about the details.

Life. That sentence says it all. In my father's case, fifty-two years was "life." That simple. It was such a strange thing to process. We didn't talk about it at home at all. It's not that my mother refused to discuss it; I'm sure she would have. I just didn't know where to start, and there are certain things you just have to chew on until, at last, you're ready to give them voice. Few kids at school knew what was going on, and everything involving my father happened in the far background of my life. Shortly after the police caught my father, my football coach called me into his office and asked me how I was doing. He told me that I needed to stay on my path and that I would make my family proud. But that was all the acknowledgement I ever got that something unusual had happened. There simply were no counselors, no uncles, no mentors, and no one to talk to.

Oddly, my father's fate was a weird type of motivation. When I heard about the sentence, it hit me like a punch to the gut. I thought, *Man, he's going to die in there.* But then it dawned on me. *We're all dying.* You're given a limited time in this world, in this life. So it's wise to ask yourself what you want to do about it. Everybody's going to die. We're dying right now. The real question is, Who's going to live, right now, a full, meaningful life? It renewed my commitment not to make the mistakes my father and his father before him had made. I was determined, more than ever, not to be a victim of legacy, not to be trapped by the hood but instead to be who God destined me to be.

Today my father still sits in that prison. But what about all of us in our own prisons? For many of us, that's what we choose. There might not be metal bars or orange jumpsuits, but we keep ourselves locked in the prison of other people's expectations. Or we look across the street and put ourselves in the prison of wanting what those people over there have. We imprison ourselves in debt. We stay in our prisons because they're comfortable and don't challenge us. My father was one more reason for not choosing a prison of my own. There was nothing else I could do with the knowledge of all that had happened to him other than let it propel me forward.

In the spring of every year, Verbum Dei had an assembly that the entire student body attended. It was meant to inspire; the senior class dean got up on stage and announced which colleges each senior was going to attend. I was a freshman, sitting in the second row, when I heard that one of the stars of the Verb basketball team, Doug Mills, had gotten into Stanford on an academic scholarship and would continue playing basketball there. I knew Doug. He was smart, certainly, but I never thought of him as super scholarly. He was a talented athlete and personable. A low-key guy with a lot of swag. I felt like I worked every bit as hard as he did in the classroom, and

I had my own athletic skills on the football field. I had potential and I knew it.

I turned to the kid sitting next to me, the first Afro-Panamanian I had ever met, Jared Sanchez, and said, "Hey bro, I'm going to go to Stanford too."

He smiled broadly at me and nodded. "I feel that, bro. We're doing it together."

I always knew that college was going to be part of my path out of the hood. But up to that moment, sitting in that electrified Verbum Dei auditorium, it had never really sunk in that kids from the hood could go to a place like Stanford. I realized that there was nothing standing between me and an elite university if I just worked hard enough. Doug Mills was what it looked like when you handled your business in the classroom and reached out to grab opportunities.

Stanford was just a name, nothing more than a notion of what could be. At a school college fair, a representative from the Baylor University booth handed me a T-shirt as I walked by. It got me thinking. Baylor was a competitive Division I football school with a strong academic program. The next year, they had a stunningly talented quarterback named Robert Griffin III. The first time I saw him on TV, in a game against Texas Christian University, I texted my Verbum Dei coach. "Coach Troy, I don't know who this Robert Griffin III dude is, but I guarantee you he wins the Heisman." And sure enough, he did. Baylor rose to the top of my college picks. But Baylor's opponent in that game had made an impression. The purple-and-black team that lined up across from Griffin had played tough and made Baylor work for the win. They were the real deal, and TCU stuck in the back of my mind.

At our end-of-season football banquet in January, we had a guest speaker who changed my understanding of what I could do as an athlete. His name was Stafon Johnson, a star running back at USC. Stafon had gone to high school in the heart of a neighborhood literally called "the Jungles." It was the neighborhood featured in the movie *Training Day* with Denzel Washington. It was awe-inspiring to be in the presence of a hometown hero. I don't remember anything from his speech except that toward the end, he looked in my direction in the crowd and said, "Anyone can make it to play ball in college, even him."

At the time, I was one of the smallest players on the team, at five feet three inches tall and just 114 pounds. I looked behind me to see if he was talking to someone else, and no one was behind me. I didn't receive any trophies or awards that year during the banquet, but I walked out thinking, *Wow, Stafon Johnson said that I can play college ball. It is possible.* That boost of confidence was better than any award I could have received.

I spent the rest of the year honing my work ethic on and off the field. I was determined to become a combination of what I got from Doug Mills and Stafon Johnson. I filled the rest of that second semester with weightlifting after school, then hung out with my crew on the weekends. A new dance phenomenon, called Jerkin', had become popular in 2009. It was rumored to have come out of Long Beach Polytechnic High School, and was then made popular at Hamilton High School. The main dance moves consisted of the "reject," "jerk," "yahh dance," "dip," and "pin drop." As for the attire, it was popular for people to wear skinny jeans, Vans, long-sleeved flannel shirts, and snapback hats. We would go up to the Del Amo Mall, Fox Hills Mall, or Baldwin Hills Crenshaw Mall with the intent to battle another crew, making dancing videos and daring each other to ask for girls' AOL Instant Messenger emails and phone numbers.

Once I made varsity in the summer of my sophomore year, I stopped hanging out at the mall. I was all football and school, 24–7. Even after I became the starting quarterback my junior year, I never spent a minute thinking I could slow down the pace of work. My junior and senior years entailed waking up at 5:00 a.m. every morning and turning on Meek Mill songs and Eric Thomas speeches. I liked to listen to Meek Mill because in his rough lyrics about crime and poverty, I heard him talking about the same things I saw when I walked outside my house. At the same time, he talked about being a dream chaser. Eric

Thomas, whose videos I found on YouTube, gave inspirational speeches about dream chasing as well. These two voices were the soundtracks to my life during those years. I woke up early to do my pushups, pray, and then hop on my bicycle to head to the 24 Hour Fitness gym in Compton to work out, or to ride up to Compton College to run the bleachers. Leaving the house so early felt safer, because I assumed that all the gang members had to sleep at some point. Those early morning hours were the only times that gang activity was dormant. I knew I would safely get to my destination. The words that I recited to myself from Eric Thomas's speeches and Meek Mill's songs on those long bike rides were my confirmation to myself that I was going to get to my next destination: college.

The more I thought about college, the more excited I got. I threw myself into the application process. I didn't consider any college out of my grasp. The only thing that limited me from applying was time and circumstance. As I got closer to the application deadlines, it was a challenge to juggle schoolwork, workouts, my work-study commitment, and the logistics of home life. The more crunched for time I got, the more I had to use my grandma's computer, and that became an issue. I had applied to all the schools I was attracted to except five on the top of my common application list. I was working on my grandma's computer, trying to complete the applications online, when she told me to get off the computer because she wanted to do some online gambling.

"Grandma, no. This is really important. I need to do my college applications."

"College? I don't care about none of that. A real man works with his hands."

It was an all-too-common reaction where I'm from to anyone with big dreams.

"I don't wanna hear none of that. I'm trying to go to college."

"You get off my computer." I could tell she was getting angrier and angrier as I tried to ignore her and focus on finishing the application that was up on the screen. Finally she said, "You think you big and bad now? I got something to cut you down to size." And off she went to get her gun, a .22 that she kept in her closet.

Most households in Compton probably have a gun, and the thinking is that a person needs to be willing to use it or there's no point in owning one. The point is respect, confronting perceived disrespect, and keeping what little you have even if it means doing the unthinkable. My grandma went to her bedroom to get her gun, and as strange as it may sound to someone who isn't from the hood, she might have shot me if I hadn't got off that computer. I hoped that she was just trying to flex her muscle with that rusty old "deuce-deuce" in her hand. But growing up you always heard the saying, "Never pull a gun out if you don't intend to use it." The mind-set in the hood was that to let anything go is to let everything go. I wasn't going to call my grandma's bluff.

I got up and went out to the garage, where I slept on the floor because I had grown too tall for the bunk bed Chase and I had moved to when I started high school. I would end up missing the application deadlines for those last five colleges. As I sat on the edge of the worn mattress processing that reality, I couldn't stop the frustration from welling up. You could work so hard and still have those closest to you stand in your way. There was an injustice to life in the hood. But I knew better than anyone that there was simply no point in complaining about injustice. It just is.

I started to think about how someone in the hood could work as hard as they could, try their very best, and still, if they didn't "make it," people would assume it was because they were lazy and taking advantage of the welfare system. It ticked me off that if my grandma shot me, people would never know my story or what I had to go through for a better life. As the frustration ate at me, I began to cry and let the tears flow until I could gather myself for what came next. More schoolwork. More workouts. I had to remind myself that the path God gives you is about how God believes in you. The toughest battles are reserved for the toughest soldiers. I also kept in mind that the race is not won by the swift but by the one who endures to the end. Tough times don't last; tough people do. I took a breath, wiped my tears, blew my nose, and got on the floor to hit my pushups. I told myself that one of those pushups would be the one that would take me out of this situation.

I would eventually apply to forty-five colleges and get accepted into thirty-six, including UCLA and Boston College. But getting in and being able to pay tuition were two entirely different things. I had to be even more energetic chasing scholarships.

As we saw it in the hood, the easiest way to finance college was with a full-ride football scholarship. It's an all-in-one ticket. My problem was weight. I had good stats on the field, but at 165 pounds I was just too light for many college recruiters. Even when I was in high school, we were still struggling financially as a family. Dinners were often one item off the McDonalds' dollar menu. As an athlete burning calories like crazy, I needed more food to put on the weight that would impress college scouts.

I would scrape together the money for a four-pack of Ensure from Rite Aid, since we couldn't afford real protein. I figured that people in the hospital drank Ensure as an entire meal, so I could drink one before going to sleep to pack on some pounds. Sometimes I would get frustrated that my mom couldn't provide enough food for me to chase my dreams. But I never complained when she told me that she had to prioritize feeding Mi and

Chase, and that I wouldn't have enough for dinner to be full. Instead, I would drop down on the garage floor and transfer those searing hunger pains that were in my stomach into my arms and chest through pushups. I often slept on the floor in puddles of sweat.

The coach from Colgate University came and sat in my living room, said all the right things, and told me he'd love to have me in the football program. A week later, thinking I had a place at Colgate, I got a call from the coach, who told me that they had filled the last scholarship slot and had to rescind the one that they offered me. I learned that this is what happens in college football. It was frustrating, but it was the reality.

I told myself, *No matter what, I'm going to college.* I discovered that if you're resourceful, you can string together smaller academic scholarships that could conceivably cover tuition. I was determined that however I needed to write the ticket, it was going to happen. I applied like crazy and managed to land a string of smaller scholarships that would help ease the way. They ranged from a Friar Tux Shop scholarship ($500) to the Los Angeles Urban League–Mattel College Scholarship ($5,000). I was even awarded a Children's Defense Fund (CDF) scholarship ($10,000; $2,500 per college year). The CDF is a nonprofit started by civil rights activist Marian Wright Edelman, the first black woman admitted to the Mississippi Bar.

As part of granting the scholarship, the CDF films documentaries of the recipients as profiles to inspire other kids in inner-city areas and impoverished circumstances. At first I was reluctant. I had never told my story before. I didn't even think of myself as someone with a story. I was just a kid who put his head down, grinding and working hard. My assumption had always been that the people around me had come from similar circumstances, so there wasn't anything special about me. I really didn't like all the attention that a documentary would bring. I was afraid that it would turn some of my family against me, relatives who lived in wealthier areas in Carson and other places. I didn't want to embarrass the people in my family who were lawyers with their own firms and doctors with their own practices. People don't like to feel negligent, even when they are. When I told my mom that I didn't want to do the documentary, she was very clear on why I should.

"Look, Caylin, God has a special plan for you. People will know your story. So it's either you tell it from the perspective of a victor, or let them tell it, and they'll make you out to be a victim. They will make something that is so beautiful into something that is so ugly. Unless you tell it yourself, nobody will understand the intricacies."

I hadn't considered any of that, but it sure made sense. "Yeah, that's real. All right, I'm going to tell my own truth."

The film crew showed up at school on a Thursday in October and put a mic on me. They followed me around, and the next day they interviewed me a few different times. On Saturday they came and filmed our football game. Then they went away, edited all the footage they shot, and put the film up on the Children's Defense Fund website and YouTube. I received positive feedback from teachers, counselors, and other students who saw the film. That changed my perspective on the shame I held about telling my story. I realized that it was important to tell my story, not for my own sake but for someone else's.

Getting independent scholarships like the CDF's didn't mean that I gave up on trying for football scholarships. Even though some colleges might have given up on me, I kept doing what I could, emailing coaches and staying in contact with as many as possible. In December of my senior year, I went on the only recruiting visit I would have out of high school—a trip to Marist College in Poughkeepsie, New York. The three-day trip was an eye-opener. Before that, I had never heard of the college, but it turned out that Marist was a beautiful school nestled in scenic hills along the Hudson River in Upstate New York.

The school assigned Marist football player Travis Lock to be my host. Travis was a black kid from Long Island. He was a tall, muscular running back with his own big dreams that would eventually take him beyond

Marist. I roomed with him during my stay and he showed me around. I got to sleep in my own real bed for the first time since I was six years old. Even though it was Travis's bed, it seemed so luxurious. They gave me money for food, and I ate at Boston Market for the first time, ordering so much food I thought I was going to burst. I sat with the coach and talked about how I knew I could put on weight if I had a more regular diet, and how devoted I was to excelling on the field and in the classroom. I could tell he liked what he heard.

The first night, Travis asked me, "You want to go party?"

"Nah, I'm good, man. I don't party."

"You sure?"

"Yeah, I didn't come here for that. I could party back at home. I'm coming to college to handle business."

All I really wanted to do was soak it in, enjoy the food and the company of guys who would be my teammates. I remember sitting around a table with about six of them in the college cafeteria, just eating and talking. The food was tasty, and the cafeteria was clean and comfortable. The whole experience felt good. It really seemed like Marist could be the next step for me. I knew I could thrive at the college, and certainly on the Marist football field, if I was just given the chance.

The coach invited me onto the team before I left. The school was technically a Division I-FCS school. It was a nonscholarship conference, so there would be no football full-ride scholarship. However, coaches and schools at that level are adept at throwing together financial aid packages that deliver many of the benefits and coverage that a scholarship would. But as much as you might dream your dreams and make your plans, you take God's bounty as it is provided, and you're thankful. So I was grateful that I made it to college even if it wasn't an Ivy League school, or one among the many on my dream list. No matter what, I had a feeling inside that Marist was just the beginning. I knew I would have other dreams, and I knew God had big plans for me.

That kind of understanding, the lessons that life teaches you if you listen, was something I collected and kept. At the beginning of my senior year in high school, I had begun compiling what I called my "book of wisdom." It was just a plain notebook, like all students use. It had a black cover with an NBA logo on it. I filled it with lessons I learned or wisdom I overheard people in my life say. By the end of my senior year, I needed a new notebook. Now I have a shelf of them, and I continue to gather that knowledge. I look forward to passing them down to my children one day.

I knew if I was going to be an agent of change, someone who could switch up the narrative of Compton and places like it, the wisdom I collected was going to be crucial. And I knew I'd need every tool I could grab to affect that legacy—the intractable generation-to-generation pattern of poverty and hopelessness that has plagued inner-city neighborhoods for so long.

The inner cities of America have fallen by the wayside, into perpetual cycles of crime, poverty, and low educational achievement. The people who live in underserved communities are the ones who are most affected and marginalized, although they did not start these cycles. Changing the narrative and legacy in my community undoubtedly starts on an economic and especially an educational structural level. However, on a personal level, I had to begin with changing the legacy of my last name.

My grandfather, Louis Jeffrey Moore, abandoned my father and grandmother when my father was a child. My father, in turn, was a misguided man, an absent parent, and ultimately a felon who continued the downward spiral. That will not be my narrative. I refused that legacy. I was determined that I would write a new story that would serve as an example to the next generation, a roadmap for others in my community to use in breaking their own cycles. I committed to being the father my father and grandfather never were. I wanted to leverage the discipline I had gained from academics and athletics, my unflinching faith in God, and the support of my family and community to be a better husband, a better parent, and a better man.

Those three tools had been threads in my life for as

long as I could remember. But they all came together for me in the most tangible way during my years at Verbum Dei High School. I knew they would serve me just as well going forward, to college and beyond.

These are the important things I hoped to pass on to my children. My *Book of Wisdom* is a hammer that will help shatter the chains of my name's legacy. It's a new legacy for my children, and perhaps for others in my community. But it was only a start. My father was a barber, and no one in his family had gone to college. As my time at Verbum Dei came to a close, I looked forward to breaking that part of my legacy as well.

5

QUESTION: *"How will you make the most of this opportunity?"*

I knew my education would continue after Verbum Dei, but midway through my senior year it was still unclear where. Applying to colleges had been frustrating, with a lot of empty promises and disappointments. During the spring of my junior year, I had been pulled out of class on different days by the coaches of Penn, Princeton, and Dartmouth. They all said nice things about my academic record and football potential. They all said how much they would love to have me in their programs. Then, one by one, they all flew home and seemed to forget how to use email. I never heard from them again, and they didn't respond when I reached out.

Marist College became the most appealing option. The school was solid academically, I could play football there, and, most important of all, I would be able to get out of Los Angeles and grow as a person while away from home. I liked the students I had met, and the campus was pretty and charming. Even though I had been accepted to more prestigious schools like UCLA and Boston College, meeting the tuition and expenses for those schools wasn't going to be possible, even with the scholarships I'd won and adding in whatever I could make working at a part-time job. At Marist, the combination of financial aid and scholarships would cover my tuition, books, lodging, and food, just like a full-ride scholarship. I wouldn't have to work and could focus completely on school and football.

That was important to me, because I wanted to go get it when it came to college. I was just as driven as I had been at Verbum Dei, if not more. I treated all educational opportunities—whether it was Marist, another college, or later, the Rhodes Scholarship—as apprenticeships in life. I always saw them as ways to gather practical knowledge, life lessons, and worldly experience that I could bring back to my community. All educational experiences were going to translate to full pages in my *Book of Wisdom*. It didn't matter where, or when, or what the opportunity for learning was. If an "old head," a term to denote one of my elders, had some wisdom that he learned in politics or in prison, I wanted to know. If a homeless man had a clever way to stay warm at night, I wanted to learn how he did it.

So my options came down to this: enroll in Marist or go to a larger college and walk onto the football team with nothing more than the possibility that I could earn a role and pay my way. Still, I was hesitant. Marist felt like a step down from my dreams of going to an Ivy or playing for a Division I school. Because he had always been a good source of advice and inspiration, I called Coach Tony a couple of days before the signing deadline for student athletes. Sitting in my grandma's kitchen and using a cheap gray throwaway cell phone that I had bought at 7-Eleven, I walked Coach Tony through my options. He listened patiently as I explained my thinking. Then there was a long pause. Finally he said, "Honestly, C, God is going to find you wherever you are. It doesn't even matter."

That connected. Like me, Coach Tony was a devout man of God. It made sense to me that God would still find me whether I was a dot on the map or I was the map. The size of the school didn't matter to what was really important—my faith in God. I would make it work with God's help. I would realize my dreams with God's grace and hard work, regardless of where I was learning. I enrolled at Marist.

Graduating Verbum Dei was a milestone, but I didn't see it as a great occasion because I knew bigger opportunities and challenges waited for me just over the horizon. But that perspective was unusual. High school graduations in the hood can be big, extravagant affairs. People drop a lot of money on a graduation party. They'll have a DJ playing rap, a portable floor for dancing, and lots of food. They'll invite everyone they can think of. They do the same thing with their prom. I've known people who had a huge prom party and a rental sports car but a month later didn't even graduate. I had no interest in that. To me, parties celebrate culminations, the end of something or big achievements. I wanted to set a new standard for my family and the youth in my community that graduating high school should be an accomplishment no greater than graduating kindergarten. I wasn't done; I had just gotten started. There was a lot of work to do and goals to achieve.

I arrived on the Marist campus for summer football camp three weeks before classes started. The facilities were not what I had imagined a college football program would have. We practiced on a large double field close to the Hudson River. You couldn't beat the view, with the flowing gray-blue water on one side and the forested, low rolling hills all around us. But the field itself was covered in goose poop and was in pretty bad shape. Our main locker room was located under the football stadium. But because the football team shared the locker room with the lacrosse program and the men's and women's soccer teams, for our summer-practice locker room we used a large, converted toolshed. It was a plain, weathered-plank building with bare bulbs hanging from the ceiling. There was no ventilation. The wet pads and dirty practice cleats got ripe quick in the New York humidity and made the shed stink to high heaven.

It didn't matter where I put on my pads, though; playing on the college level was a serious step up. The practices were challenging. Just like when I moved from youth football to Verbum Dei, I learned a new, much more complex playbook. I had been recruited as a quarterback, and every day brought new skills for me to master. I learned how and when to call audibles if I saw a defensive front I didn't like. I learned to read defenses at a higher level, seeing potential problems at a glance and picking out weaknesses I could exploit. Like many players before me, I "redshirted" that first year. That meant I couldn't play in games, but I could practice and hone my skills on a daily basis. The year would not technically count as a college football year, so I could play a year after I was a college senior.

Coaches redshirt players to give the athletes a chance to mature, both physically and skill-wise. There's a lot to learn in making the jump from high school to college football. I was also coming in at five foot, eleven inches tall, weighing just 165 pounds. I was small for a college squad, and still growing. I knew that once I had the consistent calories of a college meal plan, I could quickly bulk up. And, in fact, by the end of my first year, I had gone through a growth spurt and shot up to six foot one. Thanks to Marist's dining hall and unlimited access to the weight room, I would end my first year at 203 pounds of muscle.

The biggest changes made in my life by going to Marist happened off the field. Getting to school early with the rest of the team meant moving into a dorm room. For the first time since I was six years old, I had my own real bed all to myself. But the most incredible difference was the bathroom. That first morning, I went to wash my hands. I twisted the left knob and hot water came gushing out. We didn't even use the left knob at home because we didn't have hot water. We didn't even have knobs. They had broken off years ago and were never fixed by the uncles or "men" in my life. I had become accustomed to washing myself through a process called a "bucket bath." I'd fill a large plastic bucket from the hose outside, bring it in, and boil some of the water. I'd wait for it to cool a little, then slowly pour it over my head as I stood in the tub. But here, all of the sudden, I had hot water on demand. Showers whenever I wanted one.

I got teary-eyed in that moment. I thought, *Wow, I'm living in this warm, cozy environment. I got my own bed, and all I have to do is turn a handle and hot water comes out. Like it was nothing.* All those years of bucket baths and pliers on the faucet handle in a ratty bathroom used by too many people. And here I was, in luxury. All the hot water I could want. I could take a twenty-minute shower if I felt like it. In that moment, I thought, *Wow, I made it. I made it big.*

As the football team was wrapping up summer camp, the rest of the students began arriving on campus, including my roommate. He was a skinny Italian kid named Alex Lupo, a laid-back surfer dude from New Jersey. His whole family—mother, father, and sister—helped him move in. They were all incredibly nice people, and Alex turned out to be the perfect roommate, even though the contrast between the two sides of our dorm room could not have been starker. His side was exactly what most people would think a college dorm room should look like: a huge poster of Muhammad Ali, a nice modern desk lamp, a flat-screen TV, and a stereo setup. He had Beats by Dre headphones and a plush cushion for the top of his mattress. His family had brought nice blankets, and he filled his wardrobe with clothes and cold-weather gear. And he had rolling plastic storage boxes that fit under his bed. The boxes were filled to the brim with snacks—little bags of Doritos, fruit snacks, and other stuff.

On my side of the room? Basically nothing. A floral print blanket that reminded me of my mom on the bed, a few clothes in the wardrobe, and a Bible in the drawer in my desk. I had my laptop, which I had received from winning the scholarship from the Children's Defense Fund, secured with a wire cord to the post of my bed. My Compton state of mind prevented me from realizing that absolutely no one wanted to steal my laptop, because everyone already had one.

The first night we stayed in the room, Alex caught me eyeballing the plastic bin of snacks under his bed.

"Hey bro, you want anything, go ahead and help yourself. Have anything you want."

I said to myself, *I love white people. Snacks galore.* It

didn't seem like it could get any better. And then classes started.

At Verbum Dei we had classes from seven thirty to three thirty. Between commuting and football practice and always being tired and hungry, there just never seemed to be enough time to properly study, to learn as much as I wanted to learn. But now I had two classes a day, four days a week. No class was more than a short walk from the dorm. I named the student meal plan the "all-you-can-eat buffet" because that's what it was for me. For the first time since I was six, I had all the food I could wolf down. Most college kids complained about the food, but it was gourmet to me. I had more energy than ever before and, with unlimited access to a weight room, I started packing on pounds of muscle. But most of all, I had time. All the time in the world to study.

My favorite class was Calculus I. The professor was an old guy who looked, talked, and laughed just like Santa Claus. I always came to math class with an open mind, ready to indulge the different methodologies to get to an answer. I liked that in math, as in many classes, you needed to be precise through and through to get to the correct answer. I had the utmost respect for the process as opposed to the product, just like I had learned from the inspirational speaker Eric Thomas. It felt good to be sitting there with sophomores and juniors and be seen as their equal. Just taking care of business at a high level.

I had all the comfort I could ask for to do my work. There was a big, beautiful library open twenty-four hours a day, and a comfortable dorm room with a respectful roommate. There were no gunshots at night, and I never had to dodge gang members or worry about hunger pains in my stomach. Halfway through the semester I realized how much I enjoyed the simple act of learning, just accumulating new knowledge and ideas. It felt like I was handling my business as I should in classes, in college, and on the field.

College exposed me to a lot of new ideas, but not all of them were worth considering. Marist was the first place I encountered athletes taking performance enhancers. Inner-city athletes don't take steroids. It's not even a consideration, because if you come from somewhere like Compton, you don't have the money for human growth hormone or testosterone boosters. And given that, as an athlete, you're already swimming against the tide of gangs and the pressures to do drugs at school, you're sure not going to start doing them for your sport.

For the most part, the black guys I met on the Marist Red Foxes hadn't ever come across performance enhancers. But many of the white kids, especially those from more privileged backgrounds, had long exposure to steroids and similar substances. At one point, I was talking about lifting weights with a teammate, a guy from Florida. He told me that in high school he had started lactating because he made the mistake of taking high-dose testosterone boosters without taking estrogen blockers. I laughed and didn't say anything, but I thought, *Dang, you all even know the science behind it! Why don't you just work harder?* The mind-set could have been the product of a generation that doesn't begin tasks and see them all the way through to fruition. Or it could be that money and access were a given in their culture, and I think those could be as much of a curse as they are a blessing.

Also, for the first time in my life, I experienced students taking prescription drugs for learning disabilities and mental health. Many of the students that I met had prescriptions for Vyvanse or Adderall. I knew this because they would openly sell the pills to one another. I was glad to hear that they were getting the help they needed. Where I'm from, learning disabilities go undiagnosed and many kids are cast aside to special education. Some parents complained that black boys were automatically recommended ADHD medication since the teachers, most of whom were usually not from the community, did not know how to interact with the children. It shocked me to learn that many people in college who needed help seemed to actually receive the help they needed. That was a foreign concept to me. Most of the time as a kid, I didn't even know help was available.

I also found it curious that such a disproportionate number of students that I encountered in college were diagnosed with ADHD. It seemed to me, if students were not taking any medication to help them focus, then they were taking other medications to help with panic attacks, anxiety, or depression. Probably because of my naiveté and lack of experience with white culture, I couldn't imagine why they were so anxious, depressed, or panicked. The only experience I had with these mental health problems was when my mom came home from the hospital.

I was concerned for my fellow classmates. A few months into my first semester, I politely asked a resident at my dorm if she could explain what people were so anxious about. She explained to me that even though kids came from wealthier backgrounds, many had internal and external pressures that caused them duress, and sometimes they didn't have the tools to deal with everything. I had never thought of it from that perspective. Her response made perfect sense to me. It made me think about my own problems, and the problems people had back at home. Back home, their drug usage was criminalized instead of medicalized. People sometimes used nonprescription drugs to deal with their problems. But they usually didn't have access to, or the money for, a good doctor, so their problems went undiagnosed and often lead to addiction. Becoming addicted to drugs, or any substance for that matter, was one of my biggest fears because of what I had seen in my community. It reaffirmed to me that I wanted to deal with my problems head-on and stay as far away from any substances as possible.

I came into Marist with a worker's mind-set. I went to a party with my roommate, Alex Lupo, the first weekend that school started. We walked up to the door together and the doorman told us that we had to pay five dollars to get in. I handed my five-dollar bill to him and walked into the party. He tapped me as I walked past and gave me a red Solo cup. I was confused, so I said, "I don't drink." Then it was his turn to look confused as he handed me my five-dollar bill back in exchange for the cup.

I walked upstairs and quickly noticed that this party wasn't my scene. I saw kegs, beers, and red Solo cups everywhere. I had left the hood to get away from this stuff. I had zero interest or curiosity in the party scene. I shook a few teammates' hands and then slipped out of the party inside five minutes. I walked back to my dorm to watch rap battle videos on YouTube.

Many people knew me at Marist, and I spoke to a wide range of people while walking around the campus. I became popular to talk to and sit with in the dining hall. I'm not sure if it was my Cali swag or the way I talk with my hands, but for some reason people were drawn to me. At the same time, though, they knew that I was a little bit different. Outside of football, you could only find me in three places on campus: the dining hall to pack in some extra calories, the weight room for a late-night lift, or the library the rest of the time, studying every chance I got. I was cool with my teammates, but we never really got close. During the daytime we lived similar lives with academics and football. But during the night, we lived differently. I didn't waste any time on video games, hanging out with girls, smoking, drinking, or anything that could derail me from my path. I was focused on becoming something. I was a man on a mission.

After I settled in more on campus, I made some friends who were also on missions. One evening I was talking with some basketball players in the dining hall. A student named Jesse Daniels was sitting at our table. He wasn't on the basketball team yet, but he had aspirations of walking on and making a splash in the NCAA. As the rest of the table cleared out to go play video games, Jesse and I stayed seated. He asked me where I was from. I told him I grew up in Los Angeles, in the Compton area. In a thick New York accent he said, "Word! Yo, that's wassup! I'm from Harlem. Pardon me, I'm from the Polo Grounds Projects, Harlem, USA."

We began to discuss the convergent aspects of our backgrounds, such as me sleeping on the floor and Jesse as a youth sleeping on a broken box spring. Jesse, who stood about six foot four, had some of the biggest calf muscles I had ever seen, and that evening we met he told me how his legs became so strong. He lived with his grandma on the twenty-fourth floor of a building in a large housing project. His building, called the "Vietnam Building" by its residents for all the violence that occurred there, had gangs on every floor. One floor might have a Blood gang and the next floor above a Crip gang. The Crips controlled the elevators for most of the year, and during the night they often would shut off the power in the elevator. If Jesse was late coming home—after shooting hoops at Rucker Park, for example—he would need to run up twenty-four flights of stairs to get to his grandma's unit before the nightly storm of gunfire began. Given how similar our backgrounds were, I was inspired by how Jesse wanted to leverage his education and his athletics to be a beacon of hope for the hopeless in his community. Just like myself.

My closest friend on the football team was Matthew Semelsberger, who we called "Semi," pronounced like *semi-automatic*. Semi had wild dark brown hair reaching down to his back and eyes that were so deep and sunken that I could never tell if they were blue or green. Semi was our starting strong safety. Most players on the team were afraid of Semi because of the vicious hits he would give on the field and because of the reckless disregard for his body that he played with. Also, Semi was on a mission to be a professional mixed-martial-arts fighter after college, and people knew that he had lethal hands and feet. On the field, his game was tough and unrelenting. Off the field, he kept to himself and was very humble. I first talked to Semi while dragging my feet leaving the locker room after a November football practice. I wasn't excited to walk through the snow to get to classes. We started talking about the completely different worlds we came from and yet how our lives overlapped in our love for God, sports, and helping people. He was from Ijamsville, Maryland. In his hometown people love hunting, dirt-bike riding, and anything pertaining to the outdoors. Semi ended up inviting me to his home my freshman year. As we got closer to his home, I saw Confederate flags for the first time in my life at a local rally. I asked Semi what he thought about the people wielding the flags. He said, "Don't worry about them, bro. If they knew better, I'm sure they would do better." I followed his advice, and we never ran into any trouble while I was there. Semi and his family welcomed me into their home and their lives as if I were blood family. For the first time in my life, I felt what it was like to sit down at a table for dinner and be surrounded by love.

As I closed out my first semester, I realized that everything I had experienced at Marist was part of my path, part of my growth. As much as I thought about schoolwork, I also thought about my evolution as a man, as a person. At the end of the semester, I flew home for winter break. I slept on the mattress on the floor of the garage, as I had for the last two years of high school. After I fell asleep the first night, I had a vivid dream. In the dream I was a lion, although I didn't realize it at first. I walked into a barbershop that looked a lot like the shop my father had worked in when I was a little boy. A red-and-white-striped pole outside, a row of mirrors in front of old, black leather swivel chairs, and barbers in their white jackets. They looked shocked when I walked through the glass door. They stared at me as if I were crazy. I just looked back at them as if they were crazy.

One of the barbers asked me, "What are you doing here?"

I sat in one of the chairs and said, "Whatchu mean? I just came to get a cut. How many heads you got?" That was how people in the hood asked how long the wait was.

He shook his head. "Nah, we don't do that here."

"What do you mean?"

He handed me one of the round mirrors barbers give customers to check out their haircuts. I looked into it and saw that I had a lion's face and a huge, impressive straw-colored mane. He said, "You a lion. A lion never cuts his mane. A lion knows who he is."

I awoke startled, breathing rapidly, my pulse pounding. I went and woke up my mom.

"Mom, I just had a dream. I'm going to get dreadlocks." I described the dream to her, but she wasn't trying to hear that. She said, "When your dad wanted to get dreadlocks it was because he didn't want a job. To me, someone with dreads is someone who doesn't want a job." For me, the logic she used missed the point. She was accustomed to the conformity of Verbum Dei and I think she connected the rigid dress code, the way all the students looked the same, to my success. She told me, "No, don't do that."

But it didn't matter. It was clear to me that the dream was a sign. One of the few fond memories I had of my dad was asking him to cut a lion into the hair on the side of my head when I was about five years old. He was a talented left-handed artist and barber, and he did it. The dream tied everything together. It was a matter of me understanding who I was as a man of God, and who I was as a black man. What I had on the inside—the heart of a lion. The dream told me that my physical appearance was as irrelevant as the stereotypes people would apply to me because of my beautiful dark brown skin.

To an outsider, it might seem strange that someone from an inner-city community can become a slave to outward appearances rather than developing their character, their inner lion. Some people might focus on the shoes they wear, the brand of belt they have on, rather than how strong their faith is and how true their belief in themselves is. But for me, as someone who grew up in the hood and was also educated in the best institutions the white world had to offer, it was totally understandable. It made sense if you factored in the notion that my people had spent more time in this country in slavery than out of it, enduring the long periods of economic deprivation and centuries without political agency, struggling through dilapidated school systems and untold years of unfair housing practices. If you understand the terms *reconstruction*, *lynching*, *gerrymandering*, *redlining*, *white flight*, *gentrification*, *crack epidemic*, and *mass incarceration*, you can easily understand how someone might try to display the little bit of pride that they have left in their choice of shoes and by wearing a flashy gold chain.

I wasn't going to follow that path. The dreads weren't about the hair follicles growing out of my head. I couldn't have cared less, to be honest. I could have cut my hair off and not thought twice about it. It's bigger than the hair. The act of growing dreads started me in the practice of not worrying about other people's expectations. I am the lion, and the lion walks his own path without fear. That's a matter of faith.

At Marist, I got strong in my faith. Every Sunday, I would walk the two miles to the closest church, Beulah Baptist. Through snow, through rain, through cold. It didn't matter. I had to literally walk with Christ in my heart. I was thirsty for my faith, for that living water, so I walked. My faith and my upbringing gave me a sense of pride that spilled over into everything I did. I had been raised by an intelligent black woman who taught me that I came from kings and queens. She taught me that no one could make you feel inferior without your permission. I don't feel superior to anyone, but I'm no one's inferior, and nobody can say anything that changes that.

I brought that perspective to my summer job after my freshman year at Marist. I wanted to expose the youth of my community to a sense of pride and confidence in themselves as intellects and future leaders. I wanted to reach youth who were subject to environmental circumstances out of their control. The Children's Defense Fund needed a middle-school reading and comprehension teacher for their inner-city summer school program they called Freedom Schools. I applied online and went to job training at the University of Tennessee and the CDF Alex Haley Farm. I spent the summer teaching eleven-, twelve-, and thirteen-year-olds a reading comprehension course at Hope Freedom School in Inglewood, California.

More than ever, the experience left me with the desire to fulfill all my potential and to gain something I could bring back to my community. I wanted to achieve things that would inspire kids in Compton, Watts, Inglewood, and beyond. So at the start of my sophomore year, I put on my best shirt, tie, and ironed slacks, and went to every office on campus—extended education, accommodation services, janitorial services, even special education. I gave every person I met the same pitch: "Hello. My name is Caylin Moore. I am an African American male from the inner city. Do you have any opportunities for me to better myself?"

The people I met were uniformly surprised at my request. I'm positive that they had never run into someone with the type of mind-set I had. Most couldn't offer anything, but I finally came to the graduate school and scholarship office. I walked in and gave the receptionist the same pitch. She sat there, surprised, and then started to laugh nervously. When she realized I was dead serious, she stopped laughing.

"Wait right here. I'll go see if Pat Taylor is in." She walked back into a warren of offices and came back a minute later.

"I'm sorry, she's at lunch."

"When will she be back?"

"Probably around an hour and a half."

"Perfect." I sat down across from her. I don't think she knew what to make of me. But after all those offices, all those rejections, and now being so close to someone who might be able to help me? As I sat there, I fought back tears. I thought about how far I had come. I thought about my refusal to come back to my community, a community in dire need of help, without anything to bring them. I thought, *If this lady thinks I'm leaving this office without a packet of something to apply to, she has me confused with someone else.*

After an hour, Pat Taylor, the scholarship and fellowship adviser, came back from lunch. I introduced myself and told her what I was there for. She invited me back to her office and began looking in files. She handed me a big packet of materials.

"You're past the deadlines for a lot of things, and you

need to be a senior for others, but you could apply to the Fulbright Summer Institute . . ."

"Thank you. Give me a few days and I'll be back in this office."

The Fulbright UK Summer Institute is the undergraduate-scholarship equivalent of the Fulbright Scholarship. No one at Marist had ever been awarded a Fulbright UK Summer Institute scholarship. This scholarship would enable me to spend a summer semester at a top British university, a hint of what was to come.

I filled out the application and submitted it with my personal statement of purpose. I made it on the list of finalists, which meant a long phone interview with the selection committee panel. I made the call in the campus chapel because it seemed to me that there was no better place to keep connected to God while I was busy with the interview. They asked me a series of intellectual questions, and I answered as eloquently and candidly as possible. Finally the woman who was leading the interview asked, "Do you have any questions for us?"

"Yeah, I do actually. I have two."

"Okay."

"My first question is, 'Do you believe in miracles?'"

There was an uncomfortable silence and the sound of chairs moving. I understood. It was an uncomfortable question. The woman launched into a nonanswer. "Well, the idea of a miracle can be widely interpreted . . ."

I waited for her to finish. Then I said, "Well, I just want to let you know I'm giving you the opportunity to partake in a miracle. A true miracle."

The other end of the line got absolutely still and quiet.

"My second question is, 'Have you ever heard of the rose that grew from the crack in the concrete?'"

There was a pause, and then she said, "No, I don't think we have."

I recited Tupac's "The Rose That Grew from Concrete" for them because it was one of my favorite poems and song lyrics, and I thought it said so much about me, about Compton, and about all those people trapped in the hood. It said more than I would have been able to communicate given an hour to talk. I could tell that the poem had sucked the air out of the room. It was not something these people were expecting to hear in a scholarship interview. But it captured who I was. I wanted to be as honest and as direct as possible, so they would know exactly whom they were sending to England if they awarded me the scholarship.

After a moment, the woman came back on the line and said, "Thank you, Caylin. Thank you for this. We'll be in touch."

Two weeks later I received a life-changing email from Valerie Schreiner of the Fulbright Commission, telling me that I was a Fulbright UK Summer Institute recipient. My heart began to pound. I wanted to get down on my knees and kiss the floor and pray a huge, long prayer of thanksgiving. But I was in the computer lab and didn't want to make a scene. As I left the lab, I saw Pat Taylor walking by. I told her the news and she was elated. Then I got on the phone with my mom and we cried together. Standing outside Donnelly Hall at Marist College, talking on what in the hood we call a "trap phone"—an inexpensive, prepaid cell phone. Look how far we had come.

The scholarship paid all my expenses for two months over the summer at the University of Bristol in Bristol, England. It was amazing to pick up my passport at the post office and just leaf through all those empty pages. Nobody in my family except for an uncle in the military had a passport. It represented so much to me.

Bristol was eye-opening. The city is located in the southwest of the country and dates from the twelfth century. It looks like the picture for a postcard. But with a population of half a million people, it isn't small. Although Bristol has only been a formal university for fewer than two hundred years, the campus includes incredible Gothic buildings and stone towers that look like something right out of *Lord of the Rings*. The city and university are perched high on the banks of the River Avon. When I wasn't studying the transatlantic slave trade, I spent hours just walking around and looking at all the medieval buildings, suspension bridges, and picturesque surroundings.

More important, I expanded my worldview because I was exposed to an entirely different perspective—on America, Africa, Europe, the world, and especially the United States' role in the African slave trade. Much of what I read I had never encountered in any American textbook. It reminded me of a quote usually attributed to Winston Churchill: "History is written by the victors." I realized that my experience in the American school system—even good schools like Verbum Dei—had not given me a comprehensive understanding of America's true part in the commerce of slavery. I came to realize the truly savage and destructive things that were done in trafficking human lives in the name of something so trivial as luxury goods like sugar and tobacco. So much pain and suffering for nothing more than greed. I learned that people perverted the Bible for hundreds of years, to justify their actions in slavery as something that was mandated by God. For the most part, both slave master and slave believed in God. One prayed for more income, while one prayed for freedom. As I read more and more about what being a slave master entailed, I began to wonder if the slave master's God was the same one Jesus was praying to.

I got on the plane home with my head swimming, thinking about all I had learned and the wonderful interactions I had enjoyed with English people from all walks of life. Going back to Marist was a little bit of a comedown, but I was excited and looked forward to competing for the starting quarterback job.

I had spent my sophomore football season as a special-teams contributor. The starting quarterback was a talented fifth-year senior, and he was immovable. The most action I got at my chosen position was sporadic snaps during the season when we had already put the game far out of reach of our opponents. We had gone on to win the Pioneer League championship in Division I-FCS. I went into my junior year as a redshirt sophomore, grinding to set myself apart from the other five quarterback candidates. I felt that I was the best athlete to lead the team, but one of the first quarterbacks' meetings of the season would shake my sense of belonging. One of the coaches gathered all of us—four white, two black—in a classroom. We sat on putty-colored metal folding chairs in a semicircle around the coach. He used a whiteboard and a marker to explain some changes to the offensive strategy and playbook, and then talked about offensive priorities for the coming season. Then he decided to do a little bonding exercise.

"I want us to get to know each other better. Why don't we talk about your favorite place that your dad took you golfing?"

The other black guy in the room, Lavelle McCullers, also had dreads. I looked at the coach, thinking, *What the . . . what planet is this guy from?* I glanced over and locked eyes with Lavelle. Even though he had grown up in a two-parent household, he was obviously thinking the same thing. The white kids didn't bat an eyelash, and one jumped right into a story about a time his father took him to some nice course in New Jersey where he shot one of his best scores. I was taken aback that the coach had just assumed we all had dads in our lives, and that those dads took us golfing. The mere fact that he would ask such a thing, given that people come from varying family backgrounds, made me start questioning whether I was in an environment where I could be understood. Though I wanted to wake up the coach with a thought-provoking statement, I decided to remain quiet. Instead, I drifted off into my own thoughts about my dad. I imagined which sports he liked to play and what he might have wanted to teach me.

The idea of my father had become a test of faith for me. That second year at Marist, God had put it in my heart that I couldn't just talk about forgiveness, I had to practice forgiveness. I wrote to my father. It was a huge step for me to sit down at my dorm room desk and compose that first letter, slowing filling the blank sheet of paper in front of me. But it was rewarding when he replied. We began exchanging letters on a regular basis. He had found God behind bars, and his letters were written by a different man from the one whom I had known as a little kid, or the one who had killed a young woman with a rifle. It was a learning experience to see how people could change, how far someone could come in rehabilitation with the help of divine faith.

I kept in close contact with the rest of my family as well. Mi had gone on to nursing school and was doing well there. Chase, well, I was so proud of Chase. With all the academic struggles he had encountered, he had still managed to get into Verbum Dei. And, if anything, he was a better football player than I was. Just like I trained him to be. As a safety, he had led Los Angeles schools in tackles in his junior year. He stayed on top of his studies and wound up with a scholarship to College of the Holy Cross in Worcester, Massachusetts.

My football career had hit a high point at the beginning of my junior year, and the season ahead was full of excitement and promise. Everything was geared for a great season. I felt more confident on the field than ever before. I had studied the Marist system inside and out. I had built my skills by leaps and bounds, and I was the biggest and fastest I had ever been. I might have still been figuring out where I was going to ultimately fit as a man, a black man, and a contributor to my community, but I had no doubts about where I stood on a football field. The only thing I hadn't accounted for was that my body might betray me.

In a preseason practice on a warm August day, with puffy clouds floating low over the Hudson River, I dropped back to hit a receiver on a simple flag route. I had fired off that pass about a million times before. But as soon as I felt the football's laces trail off the ends of my fingers, my left leg went numb all the way to my foot. I felt a sharp pain in my lower back, right at the spot where I finished my follow-through. I had broken my left wrist once when I was in the Snoop League, and again in high school, but that was the most serious injury I'd ever had. Whatever this pain and numbness was, I didn't think it could be anything to really worry about. As a football player, you tend to think you're indestructible, that serious injuries only happen to other players, or pros. But as the practice went on, I noticed that the tightness in my back and the numbness in my leg were messing with my throwing action. I couldn't get any torque, so I was essentially throwing with arm power only. That made my passes slower and less decisive and messed up my timing.

I expected to just bounce back. Instead, the pain got worse and worse over the course of the next week. Finally, I made an appointment and went to see a doctor. He examined me and came to the conclusion that I had sprained my back or pulled a large muscle. I felt relieved that it was something minor, something I could fix and get past quickly. He referred me to a physical therapist. The therapist gave me stretching and back-strengthening exercises to do every day. But to my surprise, the unusual numbness, back spasms, and pain just got worse and worse.

I continued to practice, still thinking that I would wake up one day and my back would be normal again. The pain and inflexibility took its toll, and I simply couldn't perform. I had always had a strong throwing arm and deadly accuracy, and I was a good scrambling quarterback with the ability to run out of the pocket when I needed to. Now, though, I just wasn't mobile enough or able to throw to my true abilities. I fell out of competition for the starting role, and I struggled just to get through football practice and back and forth to classes. The rest of the time, I lay on the floor in my dorm room, the only position I could find that wasn't entirely painful. That's where I studied. It's where I did a lot of thinking.

The first game the Marist Red Foxes played set the tone for what my lost season was going to be like. We were taking a beating when, in the third quarter, the coach called me over.

"You ready, C?"

"I can't go, Coach. My back's locked up."

He wasn't happy about it. Neither was I. The last thing I wanted to do was let down my coach or my team. I so badly wanted to get into a game and show what I could do. I had trained so hard, through so much pain. But I knew what would happen if I got out on that field. It was going to be a bad showing, and it would be the last chance I would get to showcase my skills and abilities. I knew that I couldn't scramble, I couldn't run, and I couldn't hit a receiver on a tight route. I would have done the team more harm than good by being out on that field.

I continued working out, practicing, and trying as hard as I could to play through the injury. Sometimes the best you can do is hold on to your hope and move forward, but the truth was, I struggled to hide how badly I was hurt. Day to day, I just hoped that the coaching staff wouldn't notice, wouldn't realize how bad it had gotten. Fans and the administrators involved don't like to talk about it, but college football is like a factory. In a factory, you might have a worker stapling a part, or gluing something together, or packing the finished product. But if any given worker can't staple, glue, or pack, the factory just gets rid of them and finds someone who can. I didn't want to be cast aside.

Finally, near the end of the season, my physical therapist admitted that regardless of the different exercises he had given me, my back wasn't getting any better. He said that there was nothing more he could do for me. As I lay on the padded trainer's table in the physical therapy room, staring up at the fluorescent lights and the defeated look on his face, he said, "Look, C, this is more than a muscle or sprain. I think this is something structural."

"I'll just keep working through it. Sooner or later it's gonna get better."

"No, Caylin. This could be something serious, something with a disk. You have to go back to the doctor and get this thoroughly checked out. Guys with injuries like this, sometimes they wind up paralyzed. You need an MRI."

Paralyzed. That hit me hard. Much as I loved the game, the last thing I wanted to do was wind up in a wheelchair because of college football. I went back to the doctor and he ordered an MRI. The scan showed a bulging disk between my L4 and L5 vertebrae, and the doctor told me that the disk could be herniated. It was a serious medical problem, and no amount of physical therapy was going to make it right. He told me I would need surgery, but I decided to get through the season and the rest of the school year so that I wouldn't lose anything in the downtime.

As the season came to an end, I fell into depression. All my hard work was slipping away. It seemed like I was barely going to make it through Marist and graduate with a degree, and I would basically have nothing exceptional to bring back to my community as a message of hope. Each day was just more darkness to get through. I prayed and prayed. Finally, alone in that dorm room that had been such a comfortable sanctuary, it dawned on me that God was telling me, "Son, you need to leave. You're not going to play football here anymore, and it's time to reach beyond this place." The more I meditated and reflected, the more solid that idea became. I needed to make the moves I had to make in order to become the man I was supposed to be. I had to leave Marist, even though I had only one more year till graduation.

One day I checked my email spam folder and found a promotion for a public policy junior-year summer institute program at Princeton University. The program was focused on both domestic policy and international affairs, and would run from early June through late July. The program was fully funded—flights, food, and all. I stared at the email and the Princeton logo with its distinctive black-and-orange shield crest. I thought, *You know what? It's time to make this move happen. Princeton can be the step to whatever lies ahead.* I followed the link to the website for the program, filled out an application, and submitted it.

Just taking action, moving forward to change things, made me feel better. I felt like I was coming out of a drunken stupor, stepping out of a thick cloud. I sat at the bare desk in my dorm room, tore off a piece of paper from a page in my notebook, and wrote down "Division I Football Player" and "Harvard PhD." Sure, they looked like dreams too big to come true, but I saw them as positive, aspirational goals that I could focus on again and again if I started getting depressed. The first was from an old desire I had to have my father see me play football on TV. I told myself that I would not stop playing football until my father could see that Moore name on the back of a jersey, and see my face on the television in the Tehachapi penitentiary rec room. The second was a matter of wanting to go back to the hood and be able to say, "Hey man, I went to Harvard. I set foot on that campus and I've seen how it is. It's doable. It's possible. I love you. I'm from where you're from, I've experienced what you've experienced, and I want you to know that it is possible." At that time I didn't really even know what a PhD was. Furthermore, I didn't know exactly where Harvard was. It was a big dream, but I knew what that would mean for kids in my community.

When I received the email that I was accepted into the Princeton program, I was crystal clear on what I had to do next. After Princeton, I'd finish my time in college playing football on a Division I team, no matter what. So, late at night, after I was done with my studying for the day, I'd get to work on my computer. I'd comb through video clips from workout tapes, practice sessions, and what little game film I could get hold of. I emailed the finished training video to all the coaches I had ever had contact with—and didn't hear back from any of them. If at first you don't succeed . . . Next I sat down with a good friend named Kwame Darko, who was a video whiz. We compiled and edited a second tape. When we were done, we uploaded it to WorldStarHipHop, an incredibly popular, urban inner-city news and entertainment social media website. The video got over 800,000 hits inside a week. I started getting calls from coaches. I was getting traction. With Princeton on my calendar, and confident that I would get into another college for my final year, I went to see the Marist head coach.

"Hey, Coach. I've decided to transfer out of Marist, so I'm hoping you'll sign my release."

He was quite plainly shocked, halfway between laughing and sputtering. In the normal course of a college football career at Marist, students didn't typically transfer out. And they definitely didn't transfer out for their final year. Even if they had two years of football eligibility left. Even if they got accepted to a college—even if they got onto the football team—transferring meant starting all over, learning a new system, getting familiar with different teammates and a different coaching staff. It's just not done. But I was doing it. I wasn't willing to let my dreams just fade away. I was going to fight to the bitter end to become who I needed to become, to fulfill my potential.

"Well, I'll sign your release, C, but are you sure that's what you want? Have you thought this through? You sure you want to do this? Do you know where you want to go?"

"Yeah, Coach, I've thought about it. It's what I want. I'm not sure where I want to go, but I know I'll be all right."

"Okay, well, good luck to you."

I had the signed release papers two days later.

The interest in the WorldStarHipHop video had led to offers from Norfolk State University in Virginia and a conversation with Alabama A&M's coach, as well as contact with Texas Christian University. It was the team I had watched on TV in high school, the purple-and-black team that had given Robert Griffin III and the Baylor Bears a tough game in the 2011 season opener. I wasn't quite sure what I was going to do, but I knew I now had options. And I knew God would point me in the right direction. I prayed for guidance.

As I planned for my exit from Marist, I realized that I was going to need money for the expenses that were sure to pop up. At the very least, I would need the cost of a plane ticket, and maybe a lot more. I wasn't quite sure how far my existing scholarship funds would carry me or what scholarship offers I might get. Although I was making a little bit of money as a part-time tutor, I decided I needed to get a more regular job.

I found one in the janitorial department. At first it was a desk job, little more than filing and answering the phone. The job was ideal, because it left a lot of downtime for studying. But the woman I worked for was one of the meanest people I've ever come across. She was an old Irish woman with grayish-red hair. She was abusive to her employees, most of whom were Italian-speaking immigrants. She would yell at them and speak down to them in the most demeaning way. I also came to believe she was playing games with their paychecks and shorting them the money they were owed. Unfortunately, as much as I tried to hide it, it wasn't hard for her to pick up on my disapproval. One day I came into work and she called me into her office.

"I'm going to have to let you go."

"Why?"

"I need somebody in here with more office experience."

That was just nonsense. Not only was the job incredibly simple, I had worked at Union Bank and Shea Properties in Los Angeles. Both were fast-paced offices where I had to multitask and get things done. There wasn't anything in the janitorial office that I hadn't done many times before *and* well enough to earn me great performance reviews.

I came back to the office on Friday to get my final paycheck, and the woman who had been my boss was obviously feeling guilty about what she had done. She said, "You still need a job?"

"Yes, ma'am, I do."

She slid a piece of paper across the desk. "Go talk to this person. He'll set you up." The name on the paper was the head of janitorial services. Just like that, I went from office assistant to janitor.

I never aspired to be a janitor, and at first the reality of it weighed on me. I had a hard time seeing my new position as anything other than a great fall. I let my pride get the best of me, considering it a lowly status job. Working on campus in that role meant that my fight toward progress was made public. I was the same guy who had a documentary made about me in high school, the same guy who came into Marist thinking I would be the starting QB in two years. I carried my 3.9 GPA proudly. But now? My back hurt all the time, sometimes so much that I couldn't think beyond the pain. Now I wasn't on a football field, feeling the rush of the play and hearing the roar from the bleachers. Now I was the guy outside the first-floor common room in the freshman dorm cleaning up a puddle of vomit, courtesy of kids who partied too hard. During my freshman year I had lived happily in Champagnat Hall and had my first feelings of satisfaction over making progress for my family and my community. Now, scrubbing toilets and mopping floors, I felt like I was going in the opposite direction.

One day, one of my friends, a basketball player named Obi Momah, walked by as I mopped a hallway in the administration building. I was wearing a gray tank top, sweatpants, and brown, steel-toed work boots from Walmart. He did a double take and stopped in his tracks.

"Caylin? Bro, what happened?"

I could explain all I wanted. I could explain everything to him. But I just shook my head and shrugged. He dapped me up—that is, he shook my hand—and then he carried on to the dining hall. Just him asking me that question cut me deep. It was something I asked myself almost every day. I was losing sight of Princeton and whatever school came after that. Instead I envisioned going back home with so little to show for my years in college: nothing more than a piece of paper and broom-handle calluses. I had to get my head right.

A few days later, while I was mopping a floor outside the dining hall, a former teammate walked into the building. He was someone I had never really connected with, the type of person who might see my dreams as foolish. As he walked past me toward the dining hall he said, "Hey, you missed a spot."

I turned toward him, "Where?"

Then he spit on the floor and kept walking.

I'm human. Like any young man, I struggled in that moment with an internal battle. My fist automatically balled up from his disrespect. I could easily have beaten him . . . and created even more misery for myself. Instead, I stood there suppressing my natural instincts, the urge to answer indignity and negativity with more of the same. But I took a second and thought back to a revelation I had experienced the night before.

I called my cousin Lorne to let him know the moves I was planning to make and my situation as a janitor. Lorne was studying nursing at a historically black university, Southern University in Baton Rouge, Louisiana. He encouraged me with some of the black history that he had learned in one of his classes. He told me, "Don't even trip, bro. Booker T. Washington, one of the most intelligent

Americans of all time, was once a janitor. His exam for getting into college was based on how well he swept and dusted a room." Lorne's words were right on time. That was all I needed to hear. After I hung up the phone, I knew that there was no way that I would ever mop and sweep with my head down again.

I immediately started praying over my circumstances, asking God for the strength to make it through this challenging time. I prayed for another chance to make my city and my family proud. And slowly I realized that I was doing exactly what I needed to do. It was hard, but I had done hard, many times. And then it hit me. As I was reading, stretched out on my dorm-room bed, I came across a quote that put everything into perspective. It was something Martin Luther King Jr. had said in a speech to students at Barratt Junior High School in Philadelphia in 1967. But it felt like he was talking over the span of history, right to me.

> If it falls to your lot to be a street sweeper, sweep streets like Michelangelo painted pictures. Sweep streets like Beethoven composed music. Sweep streets like Leontyne Price sings before the Metropolitan Opera. Sweep streets like Shakespeare wrote poetry. Sweep streets so well that all the hosts of heaven and earth will have to pause and say: "Here lived a great street sweeper who did his job well."

If this was it, if my lot was to be a janitor at this moment in time so that I could go on, then so be it; I would be the best janitor Marist had ever seen.

I looked at my former teammate and called back to him.

"Hey, where are you going?"

"To the café. Somewhere you can't."

"Is that right? I'll tell you what. When you go to that café, tell them to put the food in your hands. Bring that food back from the café, put it on this floor, and eat it off the floor. That's how clean this floor is going to be when you get back here."

He walked off with a look of utter confusion on his face. But I didn't care. I was going to take pride in what I was doing. If anybody passed this spot on Marist College's campus, they would know Caylin Louis Moore had been there, because it would be spotless. It would be cleaned like it had never been cleaned before.

I kept working as a janitor, doing the best job I possibly could, until it came time to pack up what few belongings I had and take a plane home to finally fix my back. I had my back surgery in the first week of June, two days after I got home. I had an offer from Alabama A&M for a partial scholarship and a shot at the quarterback position. Still, I wasn't sure. I continued to pray to God for a sign that Alabama A&M was where I was supposed to go. I knew God had a plan for me; I just needed the next step in that plan to be revealed to me.

I went in for the surgery on a June morning at 7:00 a.m. I was nervous, but I put my trust in both the surgeon and God. I came around in recovery, and the doctor stopped by to tell me the surgery had gone perfectly. He had repaired the herniated disk and, given the physical shape I was in, he thought I could look forward to a quick recovery and rehab. It was all good news.

A few hours later, I walked out of the hospital with the help of my mom and a nurse. My mom had my cell phone in her hand because I had almost left it behind. I was still a little loopy from the anesthesia and the effects of the surgery when my phone rang. She answered it and handed it to me.

"Hey, Caylin, this is Paul Gonzalez. If you're still considering TCU, we've got a slot, and we've got a home for you. We'd be proud to have you as part of the Frog family."

That was the sign I had been praying for. Paul Gonzalez was the TCU defensive backs coach, the coach on the team's staff who covered outreach to California recruits. I thought, *Wow, I just got out of back surgery and the coach from TCU called? I'm going to TCU. God will work it out the way that it needs to happen.*

I told Coach Gonzalez that I would love to come to TCU, and we agreed to talk later about the details. I hung up the phone and felt an immediate surge of destiny and mission course through my veins. The medications wore off instantly. It felt right; it felt like the decision I needed to make. There would be a lot to work out. TCU wasn't offering a football scholarship, and even getting to the college was going to be a challenge. They had a quarterback who had come in fifth in the Heisman Trophy voting, so I'd be up against stiff competition for the role. I'd need a place to live, food, and books. There would be a lot of details to resolve. But like I always had, I'd get after it, make it happen, and check off one of the dreams I had jotted down on that piece of paper in my dorm room at Marist. In the meantime, I had to make the most of Princeton.

Princeton turned out to be a truly phenomenal experience. By the time I flew into the JFK airport for the ride to the New Jersey campus, I was ready to be in motion. I hadn't been allowed to work out for two weeks after the surgery, and it felt so good just to start moving around, which gave me the sense that I was pushing forward. Princeton was the most purely intellectual experience I'd ever had. It was the first time in my life that I had been afforded the opportunity to be a pure student—no sports, no busy schedule, no commuting. No distractions or other commitments beyond learning. Intellect is held in very high regard at Princeton, just as it was in my household from the standard my mom set. All the work I did at the

Public Policy and International Affairs Junior Summer Institute, held at the Woodrow Wilson School of Public and International Affairs, was challenging and exciting in a way I'd never experienced before. I took graduate-level econometrics, a microeconomics class infused with multivariable calculus, and a domestic policy class in which we worked together to draft a policy proposal that we took with us on a trip to Washington, DC, to present to the United States Congress.

But even in such a cerebral environment, I carved out time to rehab my back and get my workouts in. I still wanted to get on that Division I football field and play. Because of my physique, my brown skin, and the gold-tipped dreadlocks I had at the time, I stuck out like a sore thumb on the Princeton campus. But it worked to my advantage and led to me meeting some of the Princeton football players. I even wound up regularly throwing the ball with some of the receivers alongside Princeton's starting quarterback. It felt good to be free of the constant pain and be able to throw the way I knew I could.

At Princeton, I was exposed to things I had never even considered before. I had professors tell me matter-of-factly that I could earn a PhD in statistics or economics, publish ten books, and go to law school if I had the drive. I actually met people who had achieved all that, and they made it seem completely realistic. Where I came from, that was not a normal discussion about what was possible for a young black man like me. I was extremely grateful to be in that environment, to have the chance to expand my mind and be challenged in that way. It was invigorating.

As I got on a plane and headed home to Los Angeles to arrange my trip to Texas, I grew more and more excited. All I had to work out was details, just speed bumps on the way to where I was supposed to be. I saw TCU for what it really was. Not a challenge, or details, or hard work. I was used to all that. More important than any of those things, TCU was the next big opportunity in my life, and I was going to get everything I could out of it.

6

QUESTION: *"What if your organization TCU SPARK doesn't change the nation?"*

A dream without a plan is just a wish. My plan for TCU involved making a hard decision. It was either spend money on books and food, or spend it on housing. I didn't think I had the funds—even counting what I had made from my days as a janitor and the tutoring I had done sporadically—to do both. But you need a plan, so I decided I would buy a minivan and live in it until I could secure scholarship money or some other source of income that would pay for proper housing. I didn't see how having a minivan all to myself would be any worse than sharing a cold-water house in Compton with ten other people. I imagined myself coming to practice and to class every single day, giving it all I had, and then disappearing into my van at night without anyone knowing. I wouldn't tell a soul.

The hitch in that plan was that, at twenty-one years old, I didn't have my driver's license. So on a typical hot Southern California Thursday in early August 2015, my dad's brother, Uncle Massi, drove me to the Compton DMV. Uncle Massi had taught me how to drive by taking me on the I-110 freeway the very first day I was behind the wheel. Before we started up the on-ramp, he had me pull over onto the shoulder of the road. He turned in the passenger seat to face me and put his hand on my shoulder. "Drive like you've been doing this for ten years." He had me feeling confident long before we reached the DMV.

Like most of Compton, the DMV is a gritty place. I waited in the long line, studying the test as I stood there. I passed the written part with five points to spare but just barely managed to pass the actual driving test. The next day, I answered a Craigslist ad for a 2003 Kia Sedona from an older Filipino man named Gerry in Carson. It was a silver minivan with twenty-two-inch chrome rims and all the room inside that I would need to make it through a semester at TCU. I was most excited about those rims, which glistened as the sun hit them. It gave me a sense of pride in the car. I plunked down my $2,500 and got ready to drive to Texas.

Unfortunately, sometimes you have to learn the meaning of "buyer beware" the hard way.

The trip started out fine. My mom came along to help with the driving, and we made good time out of California and into Arizona. But halfway to Phoenix on the I-10 freeway, I noticed the minivan's temperature gauge was in the red. I was anything but a car guy, and my mom only had the knowledge that she had learned from her dad as a child. So we pulled into a rest stop and parked. I popped the hood and checked the radiator and discovered that it was almost dry. I had no idea what would have made a car go through all the water and coolant, but we bought a large plastic jug of coolant and poured it into the radiator. Then I filled it the rest of the way with water and hoped that I had taken care of the problem. Just finding the radiator fill cap had taken every bit of mechanic's knowledge I had. Skills like fixing a car are the types of things that you pick up from a male role model, at least where I'm from. A dad, an uncle, a grandpa, or a kind and patient neighbor. I never had men like that around me.

Back on the freeway, the minivan ran fine for about fifty miles. I was lulled into believing everything was fine. Then, out of nowhere, it overheated in a matter of a minute or so. Suddenly I heard a loud *thunk!* and ugly flames began to flicker out around the edges of the hood. I veered off onto the shoulder of the interstate as quick as I could. Gray-black smoke started spewing from the center console inside the car. My mom and I got out and acted fast, because we wanted no part of a car fire. As I rushed around to the back of the minivan, pulling out my bag of sneakers first, flames from the engine started flaring out and engulfing the front of the car. The fire grew amazingly fast. My mom threw open the side door and we grabbed the rest of my bags from inside. Then we started running back the way we'd come, both of us thinking that the minivan was going to explode like something out of a movie.

We were about a hundred yards away when we looked back and saw a big rig pull over in front of the minivan.

The fire was sending up a column of thick smoke as the truck's driver ran back toward my burning car with a fire extinguisher. He blasted the front of the car with the white spray, putting the fire out just as quickly as it had started. We made our way back to the minivan to assess the damage. The first thing I noticed was that the side of the truck was marked with two-foot-tall black lettering, spelling out "Christner Logistics." At a quick glance I thought it said, "Christ Logistics."

The driver was a short, stocky Latino guy in his forties, with close-cropped black hair, kind eyes, and a thick Mexican accent. We thanked him for his help and asked his name.

"Jesús."

I thought, *Wow, if that isn't God saying something to me, I don't know what is.* Here I had taken it as God's will that I go to TCU, and when I got in trouble along the way, who should show up to help in the midst of the fire and danger? Jesús, of course, driving a big white truck that announced who was helping me. I wasn't sure anyone would believe the story later on.

Jesús was an incredibly nice man. He offered to give us a ride as far he could go and still get to where he needed to drop off the truck's load. He let us pile the luggage in the truck and gave us a ride most of the way to Phoenix Sky Harbor International Airport. I sat in the passenger seat looking out the window, high above all the cars around us.

My mom sat perched in the sleeper area behind the front seats, next to Jesús' pet Chihuahua. Jesús talked about his family, whom he clearly adored, and his faith in God. He shared a sermon with us that his pastor had recently given about blind faith. It was like a drink of cool water on that hot Arizona day to sit next to this fellow believer and talk about our strong faith. He dropped us off at a rest stop next to a big ice machine. Along the way, my mom called a childhood friend named Jackie, who lived in a Phoenix suburb. Jackie came and picked us up at the rest stop, then took us back to her house. We stayed there overnight and, in the morning, she dropped us off at the airport on her way to work. It seemed amazing that we were just finding a way. I kept thinking, *I didn't come this far, just to come this far.* After a brief phone call back to California, my sister Mi pitched in the money for us to book tickets to Fort Worth, and we went to the gate to wait for our flight.

Once we got there and settled in for the six-hour wait, I began to panic a little. It seemed like I was just making it up as I went along, just hoping that God would have my back. I hadn't told my mom that I would be living in the van, so she didn't know that my dorm room at TCU was now a still-hot wreck on a desolate shoulder of Interstate 10. Getting to Fort Worth was going to be the easy part. I needed a place to live or I was going to be sleeping on stadium benches. I said to myself, *What if I just go back home and quit? Trade in my tickets, head back on the next flight to LA, and save myself the hardship, the embarrassment, the rejection?* Then reality hit. I'm not from a background where quitting is even an option. Quit and go where? How would I eat, sleep, and build a future for myself? There was nowhere for me to go even if I did give up. The only option for me was moving forward.

I took a breath, opened my laptop, and logged into the airport's free Wi-Fi. I checked my email. Two days before we left, I had responded by email to some listings off the TCU email blast, just in case there was a living situation I could afford that would be better than a minivan. The first email I came to was from a woman who had a three-bedroom house in Fort Worth. She wrote, "You can live here. The rent is $300 per month, and because you're a student, the first month is free." I emailed back that I'd be there the next day, and asked her to hold the room for me. Then I closed my computer and breathed easy for the first time since that minivan had burst into flames.

I was happy to find that the room was in a comfortable house with other students. A TCU undergraduate student lived in the master bedroom. A Brazilian kid who had just graduated from TCU lived in another bedroom. A doctoral student lived in the attic bedroom. We all shared the house that first semester. By the second semester, the roommates had moved on and I shared the house with the landlady—a white woman in her fifties—plus her two sons, two dogs, and two cats.

The only downside to the house was that I wasn't close to the TCU campus. That meant that I had to spend part of my dwindling scholarship money to buy another car. I bought a bland silver 2004 Ford Taurus to get me back and forth to school. But all in all, everything had come together. It seemed kind of amazing, given all that had happened, that I was actually able to attend the transfer student orientation three weeks before classes started. The orientation gave me a chance to meet a lot of other transfer student athletes, and I made some good friends among them.

Football practice started the first week of school, and my back continued to feel better and better. I practiced with the team, but I wasn't eligible to play in games. NCAA rules require that athletes transferring into a Division I program sit out a year before they can play with the team. So I studied the new playbook and worked on core-strengthening exercises. I had a lot to keep me busy, but I was hungry for game action.

The TCU Horned Frogs were heavy at the quarterback position. The starter had a solid hold on the position, and the school had given full-ride scholarships to two other quarterbacks who were pushing up on the starter. They didn't need another arm; they needed defensive backs. I wasn't sure where on defense I would be playing until the first workout. The D-back coach met me and said, "Look, if you want an opportunity to make a big impact, you need to think about playing linebacker or safety."

I like to take advantage of opportunities, so I said, "You bet, Coach." I applied the same mind-set that Uncle Massi taught me about driving on the freeway: "Act like you've been doing it for ten years." The funny thing was, I had tweaked my shoulder that week. It didn't slow me down on defense or in drills. But if I had been trying out for quarterback at that time, I would have shown badly. Much like quarterback, safety can be a very cerebral position—if a little more physical than playing offense. I discovered that I could use what I had learned as a quarterback to get an extra step on receivers and read where the quarterback was going with the ball. I threw myself into practice. That included early morning sessions in the large and well-equipped weight room.

All the NCAA teams at TCU used the weight room in the football facility, including the women's track team. That led to some fairly predictable behavior. As we waited to lift as a team, the track girls would just be finishing up and would pose a little bit, intentionally standing sideways to show off their profiles in between lifts or exercises. The football players would try to act cool, as if they weren't checking the girls out. But both sides knew exactly what was going on.

That wasn't a dynamic I was going to participate in, and I noticed one of the women on the track team was having no part of it either. She was a focused individual who would concentrate on something like power cleans, doing them perfectly. Then she'd check her workout sheet to see what the next exercise was and get busy. She was all about getting her work in. I was intrigued by her, by her focus and her ability to tune out all the distractions. She stood out from the others; she didn't waste any time looking over at the smoothie station to make eye contact with my teammates. She was obviously fit and beautiful, but she wasn't interested in making others aware of it. I noticed her, but I didn't think much more about her because I had my own work to do.

I wasn't worried that the work I was doing wasn't directly translating to on-field action. I work because that's what I do. I leave the results up to God. Because I was ineligible to play, I stood on the sidelines during games. All those guys in full gear, pads, and uniforms, and I had to stand there in sweatpants and a backward TCU hat, supporting the team however I could.

Outside of working out and studying, I connected really well with some of my teammates. During the first week of school, as I sat down in the dining hall, one of my teammates came up to sit down with me. I noticed his wild, free-form dreadlocks and laid-back attitude. He introduced himself as Michael Carroll—Mike for short. He told me his story of coming from Beavercreek, Ohio, to walk on to the team and make his hometown and family proud. He didn't make the team at first. Instead of pouting and giving up, he became a practice player for the

TCU women's basketball team to stay in shape for the next tryouts. He stayed steadfast to his mission and made the team the second time he tried out. I was inspired. After I left TCU, Mike earned a full-ride athletic scholarship during the spring of his junior year. When I met him, I had no idea what he was capable of, but I loved the way he believed in speaking things into existence. I knew right away that I was going to join up with Mike and create a "power circle" of brothers I could lean on.

In the locker room, I eventually met two more men who would become members of the power circle. In football, I mostly minded my business and spoke when I needed to. This unintentionally created an air of mystery around me. Whispers started to form about where I was from and how I got to TCU. Aaron Curry—whom we called "AC"—and Shaun Nixon wanted in on the "secret." AC was a starting defensive tackle from Del City, Oklahoma, and Shaun Nixon, from Erie, Pennsylvania, was one of our star wide receivers. They wanted to know how in the world a black dude from Compton made it all the way out to Texas. Mike, Shaun, AC, and I would always hang out outside of football. If it didn't consist of studying or lifting, you could find us "chopping it up" or having "build sessions." Those were our times to talk about life, literature we were reading, videos we had seen, or any problems we were experiencing as young black men who were trying to set ourselves up to become lights for our communities.

We wrapped up that first season by playing the Oregon Ducks in the Alamo Bowl in San Antonio. After we won the game, we all went back to the hotel to spend the night before heading back home to Fort Worth. I was still buzzing from the game and could barely sleep. I thought about the exhilaration and excitement of the come-from-behind overtime victory. Then I thought about how the day after the game would be. Would we go back to school and be patted on the back by professors, students, and people in the city? We could use the status of winners, a team that brought back a bowl trophy, to get free food from local restaurants or a phone number from one girl or another. But it struck me that we could, instead, use the momentum and energy to affect a positive change in the community. I wanted to have an impact on the youth in impoverished neighborhoods, not a free meal. I wanted to do something of worth and merit. Finally, at 3:00 a.m., I gave up trying to sleep. I sat at the little desk in the hotel room, took out the complimentary pen and a piece of hotel stationery, and started writing.

I was thinking, *Look at the energy we have coming off this win. How could we bring that back into our communities and use it for something really great?* I felt like we could harness this buzz to give hope to kids in underserved communities like the one I came from. As athletes and role models, we could guide kids onto a positive path, one where they would stay focused on their education and dream beyond their confined circumstances. The idea I struck upon was for student athletes to go out into the community and breathe life into dying situations. We could inspire the youth in those communities with our own narratives. We could become the spark for those kids to enact change in their own communities and in their own lives. Then it hit me: we could call the program SPARK. I kept toying with the letters and came up with what SPARK actually stood for: Strong Players Are Reaching Kids. Simple, direct, and powerful.

I suddenly remembered a story my mom had told me when I was very young. It was a Jamaican parable about an old man and a young boy. The old man was walking along the ocean shore one day when he spotted a boy far down the beach. The boy looked like he was carefully picking up rocks and throwing them into the ocean. The old man became curious. He kept walking toward the boy until he was finally upon him. The old man noticed that all around on that part of the beach the sand was covered in starfish that had washed up onshore. The boy picked one up and threw it back into the ocean. As he stooped to pick another one up, the old man asked him what he was doing.

"I'm saving the starfish."

"There must be thousands out here. You can't save them all."

The boy held up the starfish he had just plucked from the sand.

"Well, maybe not"—and he cocked his arm to throw the starfish back in the ocean—"but I can save this one."

I realized that SPARK might not change the whole world, but it could be a seed, a start. Sometimes you have to start with a single starfish and go from there. It's certainly better than doing nothing. So, as I wrote out the vision for the organization, I added in another aspect on the back of the paper. We would train young student athletes to be sparks themselves, to speak publicly and be leaders in their communities. One spark could lead to another, and that's how we would build a fire.

I got so excited. I kept writing and writing. A description of who would need to help us, and a list of things to tackle. Get a logo designed. Develop a mission statement that will explain the why. Draft a constitution. Contact prospective members. I wrote and wrote. Then, even though it was still pitch black and quiet as a graveyard outside, I texted Mike and AC. The texts were long, because I told them all about SPARK and what we were going to do. Of course, given that they weren't even awake yet, it would be hours before they'd text me back to let me know that they were on board.

Providence provides when you passionately pursue a good cause. Three days later I gave Mike a ride to the doctor's office to check out a knee injury he had sustained before the Alamo Bowl. Sitting next to us in the waiting room was a loquacious woman in her late thirties. She mentioned she was a teacher, and I told her all about my vision for SPARK. She lit up with excitement.

"That's such a wonderful idea! You have to come to my middle school. Can you come next week?"

Mike and I looked at each other.

"Of course."

And that became the first SPARK event. I brought six football players and the team's assistant chaplain, Coleman Maxwell. We all got up in front of the school's student body, which had gathered in the auditorium, and each of us spoke about our own experiences, influences, and the hard work that had gotten us where we were now. Our starting quarterback, Kenny Hill Jr., gave a powerful testimony of his fall from grace and his climb back to the top of college football. Kenny was a highly recruited prospect out of Carroll Senior High School in Southlake, Texas. His high school career culminated in him becoming the Gatorade Player of the Year for the state of Texas. He was recruited by Texas A&M, coming into the school in the last year that Heisman Trophy winner Johnny Manziel was there. After Manziel left, it was Kenny's time to shine. In his first game he broke the school passing record for yards in a single game and earned the nickname Kenny "Trill." As the season got a little bit rockier, Kenny ended up getting into some trouble and eventually left the university. The kids hung on to his every word and were drawn into his message that we are not defined by our mistakes. Kenny also talked about what it means to create a name for yourself, something he knew about as the son of MLB All-Star and 1994 Cy Young Award runner-up Ken Hill Sr. Another one of our teammates, a freshman on the team, expressed similar sentiments about making his own name. Rocket Ismail Jr. was the son of NFL great and 1990 Heisman Trophy runner-up Raghib "Rocket" Ismail Sr. In his speech, Rocket found a way to integrate some dance moves and wowed the kids with his energy. The students couldn't get enough. They crowded around us after all the speeches were over, firing questions at us. I wondered if we were ever going to be able to leave, but it was incredibly rewarding.

In the months that followed, SPARK kept growing and growing. I became the president and we managed to get a lot of help along the way. That first year we would do close to fifty appearances individually and as a group—at elementary and middle schools, Boys and Girls Clubs of America, youth detention centers, and even hospitals. We didn't have a highly bureaucratic infrastructure because we felt like it would detract from our mission of speaking to as many kids as possible. The structure was informal. Kenny or Mike would tell me that a local youth program reached out to them, or I would get an email from a local school, and we would coordinate a time to meet up and then carpool over to the venue. We fielded requests the best we could, given the time constraints of academics and football.

I felt like I was genuinely serving our community. I realized that we might not reach all the kids we needed to reach, but we were most certainly helping some. There was also no denying that we were planting seeds wherever we went. We were doing what Stafon Johnson and Doug Mills did for me. The kids we did influence would go on to influence other kids and other communities. We would get feedback from coaches and receive letters from teachers, talking about how quiet kids had opened up about their problems at home, and how "problem children" had started sitting at the front of the classroom and taking notes. As the months went by, I felt that we were honestly changing lives in real, substantial ways. What I didn't realize was that mine was about to change just as substantially.

I often saw the girl from the weight room around campus. I would come across her at 7:00 a.m. on a Saturday or Sunday, in the dining hall or commons. She would be studying a textbook or, often, reading what looked like a small Bible. I would see her praying over her food before she ate, which was pretty abnormal for college girls. I wondered what she was so grateful about. I thought, *Man, that's so real. Every time I see this beautiful young lady she is always by herself, just studying and focused or peacefully walking across campus to practice or class.* It struck me, too, that like me she was there early in the morning on a Saturday or Sunday. That meant she wasn't participating in the extracurricular activities of the night, drinking, or partying. I was in awe of her. I told myself, *If I ever get my act together, I'm going to go speak to that girl.*

Even as focused as I was on my schoolwork, I found myself thinking about her a lot.

After the second semester ended, I stayed at TCU to work over the summer and take some extra classes. I worked part-time as a housing department desk assistant, which mostly consisted of letting people into their dorms when they locked themselves out. It left a lot of time for studying. I had also been accepted as a McNair Scholar research fellow, which provided a $400 monthly stipend.

On July 1, I had just come back to my dorm from a workout. I was going to a church called Crossroads, which was walking distance from TCU. (Mike had taken me to Crossroads at the beginning of the school year during my first semester.) I loved how Pastor Sean Reed broke everything down so simple. I kept coming back every Sunday to get that wisdom. I was reflecting on what I had learned in church the Sunday before from Pastor Reed. I was thinking about God's will, how sometimes people forget who is really in charge and then try to take complete control over their lives. I thought about how that was a mistake. God had guided me in football and my schoolwork, and even in making the decision to come to TCU. God guided me on those long bicycle rides through Compton to get to the 24 Hour Fitness gym.

God had guided me down those dangerous streets on the way to and from school. I decided to pray. I said, "God, please bless me with an incredible woman to be in my life. Not my will, but your will be done." A half hour later, I walked outside to go to the bank, and who should I see walking down the street but the girl from the weight room with one of her friends from the track team.

I thought, *Wow, that was quick.* I jumped in my car and asked God to give me the courage to talk to this girl and not mess it up. I started the engine and pulled up next to them as they walked. Fortunately, I knew the friend that my weight-room girl was walking with.

"Excuse me, ladies, where you guys going?"

"We're heading to the bus stop so we can take the bus to Target."

"Oh, for real? I'm actually going that way. Do you want a ride?"

The truth was, going to the bank meant driving in the totally opposite direction. But my plans changed quickly, with divine intervention standing in front of me. I was so impressed that she was willing to take the bus in 2016. Most girls on that campus either had a car or were "too good" to get on a city bus. Most of them probably had never been on a city bus in their entire lives. The fact that she was all dressed up to go sit on the bus raised the likelihood that she would relate to some of my upbringing. The two of them got into the car and I started driving toward

Target. On the way there, the girl I knew asked me what I was doing with the rest of my day.

"Same old. I'm just trying to get like y'all."

"What do you mean?"

"Well, I know you all are really studious girls. You have to stay focused. That's what I'll be doing."

And for the first time, the weight-room girl spoke up.

"You're already really studious. I heard you have a 3.9 GPA."

I thought, *Oh snap, she knows I exist.*

I wasn't quite sure what I was doing when I joined them in Target. I had nothing to buy and no money to purchase anything. So, after a bit, I went to wait in the car. I got on my cell phone as they were shopping and called my friend, teammate, and SPARK partner Mike.

"Hey bro, I have a couple of girls here who want to go on a double date. They already said yes if you're up for it."

I straight-up lied to that man. But Mike got it right away and knew that coming along would help me out, so he agreed to go to the movies that night. Meanwhile, I had to convince the girls so that I could get the yes I had just told Mike I already had. As I caught up to them, I thought, *I really hope they don't say no.* And, fortunately enough, they didn't.

We drove to the movie theater that night as casual as could be and decided to see *The Purge: Election Year.* The cashier didn't hear me correctly as I selfishly asked for one ticket, so she rang me up for two. I was reluctant to pay for that second ticket because that was my money for a burger after the movie. But I handed the ticket to my weight-room girl because she was standing next to me. That's when the tide turned and we began to talk to each other, considering that we would have to sit next to each other in the theater.

We had arrived more than an hour before the movie would start. So we all decided to walk around Fort Worth's Sundance Square, a wonderful open plaza full of vendors, performance artists, water shows, and lots of places to just sit and watch everything. As I walked next to the girl I now knew as Paola, I couldn't help but think, *This is so crazy that I was just praying and God put this righteous woman in my path. This beautiful, intelligent woman with a strong character and faith.* I felt great inside. As we were walking along, we passed a man standing on a wooden crate, preaching about the holy Scriptures. Paola tapped me on the shoulder and asked, "What do you think about that?"

"What do I think about that? Hmm. Let's sit down and I'll tell you." We found a bench and sat there talking for the next hour. Best conversation in my entire life. We talked about our relationship with God, and our families and backgrounds. She was from Paraguay, and she told me about her country, her culture, and the African, indigenous, and Iberian communities of her ancestors. I told her about my city and my community. The hour disappeared as if time had no meaning. It felt like everything else around me stood still. I would have sat there a million years with her if I could have. We eventually got up and walked over to the theater to watch the movie. I didn't pay attention to a single scene. I was somewhere else mentally. In my mind, I was planning on how to court the woman of my dreams.

That one date led to other dates, dinners, walks around the beautiful Colonial golf course neighborhood. All that led to a routine that we would faithfully follow for almost a year. Every day we would meet in the dining hall for breakfast, lunch, and dinner. We never lacked for things to talk about. We discussed the deep issues of the world: race, poverty, violence, gender dynamics, family, and politics. We shared a faith, discipline, and devotion to education and improving our communities. She became my very best friend. It didn't take long for me to choose to love this incredible person.

We also shared a devotion to our sports. Paola threw the hammer in track and field and wanted to be an Olympian. I still had my last season of college football to complete, and I wanted to have an incredible year and crack the starting lineup. Although I still entertained some hope of being a one-year wonder and making the NFL, I could start to see the outlines of bigger things, of bigger dreams. The NFL might have been *my* dream, but God had something else in mind for me.

7

QUESTION: *"When did you first become interested in the Rhodes?"*

Wienerschnitzel. It's a funny name for a fast food restaurant, but it's one of my favorite places to eat. There are lots of Wienerschnitzels in Southern California, and they're also scattered throughout the South and parts of the Midwest. They're easy to spot with their bright yellow-and-red color scheme. All Wienerschnitzels serve regular fast food like hamburgers and fries, but the chain is most famous for its hot dogs and chili. I love the chili cheese dogs.

That's why in mid-July 2016 I got a friend to drive the two of us thirty minutes from the TCU campus to Grand Prairie, Texas, for the Wienerschnitzel anniversary special. Summer football camp was starting in a week, and before we started I wanted a nostalgia trip with a dollar chili cheese dog, chili cheese fries, and a chili cheeseburger. I brought my drink with me, a gallon jug of water. I needed to hydrate for camp.

The celebration ended on the way back to TCU, when a driver weaving in and out of traffic at ninety miles an hour rear-ended us. One minute we were driving along, me putting a few fries in my mouth—the next there was a loud smash, and my head whipped back and then forward.

We got out and looked at the damage. My friend's matte-black Yukon was pretty much a tank, so the other driver's Nissan Altima had the most damage. But both cars were fine to drive. Unfortunately, I had a headache when I got back to campus. A trip to the trainer told me what I didn't want to hear: I had a whiplash concussion and I'd have to go through the program's concussion protocol. That meant a week without any football activities. I would start my last summer camp almost a week late. Losing that much time training at the beginning of a football season is like starting a race two minutes behind everyone else. I never really had a chance of shining at safety. There was just no way of wrestling the starting position away from the other candidates.

Ultimately, I spent the rest of the season as a special-teams alternate and didn't get to see the field the way that I wanted to, at safety. But it was bigger than football. It was bigger than me. I would, for the rest of my life, have the satisfaction of knowing that my father had watched me play Division I football on a TV set in the rec room of Tehachapi penitentiary. That my mother came down onto the field for senior day to an entire stadium of fans cheering from both sides and shouting my name. This meant everything to me, because it meant everything to them. It had nothing to do with football. It was all about breaking generational curses for what it meant to be a black man in my family. It meant redemption. But

I became increasingly aware of the shifting of my life—the idea that playing football in the NFL wasn't going to happen.

That didn't wipe me out. I had a strange sense of relief that there was something bigger on the horizon than running full speed into people with my head and shoulders. I didn't know if it was academia, or law, or politics, but I felt like God had a greater destiny for me, something more profound than pro football. In any case, I had always understood football as a tool. My mom and my black male mentors along the way had drilled into me that even someone who is great at football, a future Hall of Famer, will go on to do something else after his playing days are done. Football was always, to me, just one more experience that would bring me closer to where I needed to be. One more experience I could use to forge myself for future challenges. One of those challenges began to take shape in the first week of the football season. I had just gotten home from a workout when I saw a text from my mom: "Don't forget to apply for the Rhodes Scholarship."

I had, in fact, forgotten. The Rhodes was part of the big packet of scholarship materials that Pat Taylor had given me at Marist. That seemed like a million years in the past. I hadn't applied then because you have to be a senior to apply for the Rhodes, and for some reason I had it in my head that I wasn't eligible for it then because I was technically on my fifth year of college. After reading my mom's text, though, I checked the Rhodes eligibility requirements and realized that I could apply.

The Rhodes is the pinnacle of scholarships, sending recipients to the most prestigious graduate program in the world. I had first learned about it in a high school history class. At the time, the Rhodes Scholarship was getting attention in schools like Verbum Dei that were located in predominantly black areas, and from students like me. The reason was Myron Rolle, an African American who won a Rhodes in 2009. Rolle was the type of singular role model a black kid could look up to and take great inspiration from. He was an exceptional individual who had played Division I football for the Florida State Seminoles and was drafted by the NFL's Tennessee Titans. He later quit the NFL to pursue a medical degree and become a neurosurgeon. Multiple teachers put articles about him in my hands. Rolle was well spoken, incredibly smart, and driven. He had a sturdy presence, athletic prowess, and a phenomenal mind. And, as I noted as a high school student, he had some swag too. So, after the reminder from my mom, I decided to apply.

Ironically, the Rhodes was founded by white supremacist Cecil Rhodes, a British diamond-mining baron who had made his fortune in South Africa while destroying many lives. He is an historical figure comparable to Adolf Hitler. Rhodes originally intended that the scholarship only be awarded to white men in British colonial nations. After his death, the scholarship evolved into a program he would not have recognized; African-descended students, other people of color, women, and LGBTQIA+ individuals have all become Rhodes Scholars since then. Among a cadre of people who want to change the world for the better, Cecil Rhodes would not have been a Rhodes Scholar.

In all of America, only thirty-two students become Rhodes Scholars each year. Two are chosen in each of sixteen different geographic districts. The competition is stiff, more so than any other scholarship I had ever applied to. At Ivy League and top liberal arts schools, students have to compete within their own schools for the privilege of becoming that school's applicant for the scholarship. I had to gather seven letters of recommendation from a diversity of sources who could speak to my academic abilities, tenacity, character, and passion to be an agent of change. The Rhodes Committees of Selection measure candidates by their "literary and scholastic attainments"; "energy to use one's talents to the full, as exemplified by fondness for and success in sports"; "truth, courage, devotion to duty"; "sympathy for and protection of the weak, and kindliness, unselfishness and fellowship"; and a "moral force of character and instincts to lead, and to take an interest in one's fellow beings."

It was hard to imagine all that winning could mean. Not only does the winner receive an all-expenses-paid graduate-degree education from the University of Oxford, a Rhodes Scholar joins a long line of people who have had great impact on the world. President Bill Clinton, Los Angeles mayor Eric Garcetti, US senator Cory Booker, and former ambassador to the United Nations Susan Rice are just a few of the extraordinary individuals who bear the title of Rhodes Scholar.

To be considered for the scholarship, I had to submit a detailed résumé and write a passionate personal essay as well as complete the in-depth application. I completed everything for the application, said a quick prayer, and then submitted all the materials online at literally the eleventh hour: 11:55 p.m. on October 5, 2016.

A couple of weeks later, I was working on a computer in the Student Government Association Lab at TCU when I decided to check my email. I found a notification from the Rhodes Committee of Selection for District 16, telling me that I was one of sixteen finalists for the district. I sat there in the hush of the computer room—the only sound the clacking of keyboard keys—staring at the words on the screen. It stunned me. I felt like I had already won. Just making it into the finalists' group was a victory for a kid like me. I tapped Paola on the shoulder, as she was sitting next to me, studying, and pointed to the screen. She started to cry. We talked about what it could mean for our community and how great God's grace was. After that, I couldn't do any more work. I needed to clear my head, to process the reality of the life-changing opportunity facing me.

I went for a walk, my mind a mess of thoughts. I must have walked four miles, just thinking and moving. Finally I stopped, sat down on a bench, and called my mom.

"Are you sitting down?"

"What is it, baby?"

"I'm a finalist for the Rhodes Scholarship."

"To God be the glory! It's God's will, Caylin. Baby, you've already won."

The news that I was a finalist quickly spread. Having a student become a Rhodes Scholarship finalist is a big deal for any college. TCU hadn't had a Rhodes finalist in years and hadn't produced a Rhodes Scholar since the seventies. All of a sudden, my email was blowing up with requests for interviews and people expressing their congratulations. But I knew that it wasn't time to celebrate yet. Rather, it was time to get with Dr. Ronald Pitcock from the honors program. Dr. Pitcock was a tremendous help while I was putting together all the components of the Rhodes application. I was looking forward to the next level of preparation. He set up mock interviews with professors from the honors program, which I thought was kind of ironic, because I was turned down for the program when I first arrived at TCU. It reminded me of when I was in first and second grade and I couldn't get into the magnet program, then I ended up beating most of the kids that were in the program in the second-grade spelling bee. But I was grateful to have the support of my university. Help is help, so I decided to see if they could provide some insight in preparing for the next step—the finalist interview.

The program set up mock interviews, but the practice sessions didn't sit right with me. Most of the interviewers kept coaching me on how to finesse my replies and how to speak like they thought I should speak. I know they had good intentions, but for me their coaching boiled down to me sounding like something I'm not. I refused to speak and act like a white guy at a 1920s *Great Gatsby* party. Probably sensing my discomfort with the contrived question and answer sessions, Dr. Pitcock told me, "I think the best thing that we can do is to let you be you." I agreed. I thought, *I'm just going to be authentically me. I'm going to go in there and be myself. My intellect, processing power, and perspective will shine. If that's not sufficient, I'm not meant to be a Rhodes Scholar. And that's fine. God will have something better for me.*

The finalists' interviews for District 16 were scheduled for Saturday, November 19, in Los Angeles. That meant missing a football game, but football paled in comparison to what this opportunity represented. A younger version of myself would have been torn, but now with more life perspective it was an easy decision. Complicating things was the fact that I hadn't just applied to the Rhodes; I had also applied to the prestigious Rangel scholarship and made it through to the finalist round for that scholarship too. The Charles B. Rangel Graduate Fellowship Program, named for the long-time congressman from New York, is focused on cultivating career US Foreign Service diplomats. The scholarship pays all the expenses for a graduate program in public policy or international affairs at a number of prestigious universities, such as Howard or Harvard. It includes living abroad as an employee of the Foreign Service, three years in one country and three years in another. It's a rare and exciting international opportunity.

The interview for the Rangel scholarship was on Wednesday, November 16, in Washington, DC. That was going to make for a busy week. If I wanted to cover all my bases, I was going to have to fly from Dallas-Fort Worth to Washington, DC, then to Los Angeles, and then back to Texas. It was going to be a whirlwind tour, but the incredible opportunities those scholarships represented made any travel or hustle that I would have to do well worth the effort. I was just going to have to do what I always did: go get it.

On that Tuesday, I caught a direct flight from DFW to Reagan International in DC. I checked into the Grand Hyatt and got to work reviewing the types of questions the Rangel interviewers might ask and what my answers would be. I turned in early to get a good night's sleep. As a group, the finalists all walked to the State Department

Annex building together. I was confident that I was as prepared as I could be to put my best foot forward in the interview.

The questions were all about international policy. What was my perspective on foreign policy in regard to immigration? How would I go about approaching the Israeli-Palestinian conflict? The scholarship is also based on thirteen qualities the committee looks for in aspiring Foreign Service officers. I had memorized the list, and I talked in the interview about each of those qualities and how they aligned with my core principles.

The second part of the interview was a timed written essay in response to a prompt question. Fortunately, my prompt was to analyze NAFTA and describe its benefits to the American economy and the potential pitfalls of the agreement. Coincidentally, I had covered NAFTA in one of my classes at TCU and was fresh with the research. I was able to provide actual statistics and case studies to back up the positions I took in the essay. On my way back to the hotel, I was confident that I had done everything possible to win the Rangel. There wasn't a lot of time for second-guessing anyway; I had to get it in gear for the Rhodes interview.

I got my luggage together and grabbed some dinner. Then I went to the airport to take a red-eye flight to LAX. My mom picked me up, but before we made our way to the hotel we stopped by some familiar places. I wanted to reconnect with the pulse of my city. Our first stop was to see my sister and to give her love and congratulations for bringing a new member into our family. I was elated to meet my newborn niece, Delanie Elise, for the first time—I had been in summer classes when she was born. She was the most beautiful baby I had ever seen in my life. I sat there for about an hour and a half, feeding her a bottle before her midday nap. I was so thankful for the opportunity to become an uncle.

Our next stop was Verbum Dei. I wanted to check in with Mr. Willis and soak up some of his wisdom. As we drove down Central Avenue from my sister's place in Carson, I noticed every crack and crevice in the sidewalk. I could hear the sweet sounds of the inner-city blues playing in the background symphony of my mind. I could hear police and ambulance sirens. I heard children laughing and I heard women crying. I heard a lot. I saw beautiful black and brown faces illuminated with smiles. I saw some kids slap boxing at the liquor store on 112th and Central. I saw raggedy buildings and decrepit schools. I saw young girls with beautiful style, attitude, and pride in who they were. I saw beauty in the struggle. I saw a lot.

When we arrived at Verb, it truly sunk in for me that the school was a diamond in the rough. I entered Mr. Willis's office and he was elated to see me. Per my usual, I immediately took out my most recent book of wisdom to take notes. The main thing that he talked about was the history of the Rhodes Scholarship. He placed things into perspective for me when he explained how big it was for my community that I was even a finalist for the Rhodes Scholarship. He explained that it didn't make any sense at all that a young black man who went to high school in Watts would even have the opportunity to apply for a Rhodes Scholarship. As my mom drove off to the hotel after we finished talking, I truly felt like I had already won, regardless of the outcome.

TCU had booked me into the Hilton Checkers in downtown Los Angeles. The hotel is right in the heart of the financial district, and was walking distance from the Los Angeles Public Library, where the Rhodes finalist interviews would be held. Coincidentally, it was also close to Union Bank, where I had worked during high school. I knew the area well and felt comfortable there. It was really good to be back home on my own turf. I felt strong, prepared, and eager to get into the interview.

First, though, there was the standard meet and greet to go through. The Rhodes Committee for District 16 held a reception that night for all the finalists. My mom and I ran into traffic on the way to downtown from Watts, so we arrived at my hotel with about thirty minutes to spare. Due to my late arrival, I chose not to check into the hotel and instead went straight to the library. I walked over to the library carrying my luggage and wearing my Nike travel sweat suit from TCU; I needed to go into the bathroom to change into a more formal outfit. While walking into the library I noticed that there were many homeless men and women outside, sitting down and talking. They asked me if I had any change or food and I told them that I would give them something when I came back out.

When I went to change in the bathroom, there were a few homeless men as well. As I opened up my suitcase and started changing, I noticed a young man with a suit on. I knew immediately that by his dress, his preparation in the mirror, and his age that he was also a Rhodes finalist. I smiled at him and said, "Wassup bro." He turned around from the mirror to see who was speaking. He looked at me opening my suitcase, decided not to verbally acknowledge me, then turned and walked away. He probably thought I was a homeless person and thus didn't see a need to talk to me. In my head I kind of eliminated him from the competition. I was hopeful that the judges would see through any pretentious displays or elitist attitudes.

The event started with an icebreaker exercise, where we all introduced ourselves, said what school we were from, and told a "fun fact" about ourselves. The first person to speak was a Hispanic American woman from UCLA. She told us her name and then said, "My fun fact is that I've been skydiving in every country in South America." The next person was a white girl from Princeton. Her fun fact was that she had climbed mountains on six different continents. Another finalist said that she had been horseback riding in the Swiss Alps, twice. It started shaping up like a competition for whose parents had more money. That wasn't a game I could or would play. When they came to me, I said, "Caylin Louis Moore, Compton, California. I'm very blessed to be here. I go to Texas Christian University, where I study economics and play Division I football. My fun fact is that one and a half years ago from this exact day, I was a janitor." I could feel the air being sucked out of the room. My resolution to be 100 percent myself shocked everyone, like a bucket of cold water poured over the head. That level of candor, that confidence, that belief in a higher mission, set a new precedent for what type of competition this would be. I was proud of what I said and the tone that it set. I wanted to take the conversation from "What have you done?" to "Who are you actually?"

After that initial exercise, we went to a catered reception, which gave us a chance to get to know the judges. I was super hungry and helped myself to a plate full of ground beef and chicken tacos. I stood off to one side to enjoy the food. As I ate, I watched. I come from the streets, where you have to be good at watching people. "Is that guy a gang member who's about to get active?" "Do those dudes look like they're trying to rob someone?" You have to develop a sense of how people move, what patterns they choose, and how they interact. People can tell you a whole lot about themselves and what they're thinking even before you hear them speak. They say not to judge a book by its cover, but I contend that you should at least read the summary to get a general idea. The summary is usually on the book's back cover. I saw that the judges were moving around the room with intention, almost in a kind of rotation. They were deliberately going from person to person, and they weren't mingling among themselves—they were only talking to the finalists.

The first judge I met was Dr. Fred E. Cohen, a professor of cellular and molecular pharmacology, medicine, biochemistry, and biophysics at the University of California, San Francisco. He was also a partner of the Texas Pacific Group, a biotech company, and a member of many different academic committees. Not knowing any of his titles or background, I embraced him like I would anyone else and had a friendly conversation.

"So I read in your application that you studied at the University of Bristol. What did you take away from your time in England?"

I thought, *Okay, this isn't something social. The interview starts now, whether we know it or not.* It was fairly easy for me to flip the switch into game mode for our conversation, given that it's the norm for me to have deep conversations. I've always hated engaging in small talk and see it as a pointless exercise—I was taught that small talk is for small minds. I would rather be completely quiet and observant or talk about something that can help us all grow and come to a higher understanding of it.

The judges kept coming up, very nonchalant, but they were asking profound questions, and I knew they were looking for profound answers. The questions themselves were well thought out and interesting to me. One of the judges had worked on President Obama's campaign and was obviously an extremely thoughtful, deep individual. She asked me about the persistence of poverty in inner-city neighborhoods. I thought, *Man, I'm just going to be real.* I spoke from my heart about the conditions of poverty, the reality of it. I talked about the constant, sometimes debilitating hunger. I told her about the soul-crushing deprivation, and the hardest battle people living in poverty face: the day-to-day struggle to keep hope alive so that they have some chance of moving beyond those grave circumstances. I gave her my realness, and I touched her soul. Judges are supposed to maintain their composure, but after listening to me, she had tears in her eyes and quietly excused herself. The real, human side of poverty has a way of doing that to people.

As the evening wore on, all those kids who had spent summers in Europe and climbed mountains on spring break kind of clustered together, like a clique. I don't think they particularly wanted to get to know me. The only finalist who showed any interest in talking to me was a Johns Hopkins student, Nicole Mihelson. She was very approachable, a nice young woman, Jewish, and down to earth. The others seemed a little full of themselves.

After I had met and talked to all the judges, I grabbed two big plates of tacos and handed them to the homeless people outside of the library. Then I called it a night and walked back to the hotel. I was trying not to be overwhelmed by the opportunity that was in front of me. I changed into my sweats and got down on my knees next to the queen-size hotel bed. I turned to the source of all my strength. I prayed a hearty prayer for focus, guidance, and that everything would work according to the Lord's plan. I prayed for the ability to communicate all I had learned and been through to the judges in a way that would move each and every one of them. When I was done praying, I slowly went through pictures of my grandma's house on the border of Compton and Carson, where I grew up. Pictures of holes in the ceiling, buckets that caught acidic water dripping through those holes, an empty old refrigerator, buckets under the sinks instead of proper plumbing, and that infamous all-purpose bathtub. I even had a picture of a trash can that I used to squat over to relieve myself as a child whenever we didn't have a working toilet. It reminded me of the struggle. I looked at other pictures of Los Angeles on my computer. I scanned through pictures of gangs and gang violence, cars shot up, and police with shotguns rounding up groups of black young men in red bandannas. I even found a picture of when the police stopped us on the Harbor Freeway at gunpoint, looking for bank robbers who ended up being in the car next to us. I looked through news articles about the hood and about the schools there. I immersed myself in my past to remind myself of what was at stake. This wasn't about me. This was something I could take back to my community. The Rhodes Scholarship could be a light I would shine for my community, something that would take me into an unknown world of hope. It would show me the unlimited possibilities that people of similar backgrounds could be provided, given that they had a village of people to intervene in their circumstances.

Then I got out my application file and reread my personal statement. I went back over my whole application and tried to think of what the committee's perception was when they read it, and what they found intriguing about it. I wanted to see things from their perspective so that I could give them the best possible answers during the interview. I thought about the questions they might ask and what I would say in response. Finally, after all that thinking and remembering and praying, I crumpled up all the paper into a ball and threw it into the black metal trash can next to the desk.

I was ready. As ready as I would ever be.

I went to bed early and slept deeply, confident that I was completely prepared for one of the most significant days in my life. I woke up early the next morning and did pushups while the golden California sunshine filled my hotel room window. I put on a tank top, shorts, and sneakers and went for a run. I ended up getting some Chinese food from Panda Express inside the public library, the same Panda Express where I ate lunch when I was in high school. I sat there getting my mind right for the biggest interview of my life.

When I got back, I showered and put on my blue Calvin Klein suit and my brown Stacy Adams wingtips, then wrapped my dreads up in a black headband made from one of my TCU practice tees. I felt like I was suiting up for battle.

Each Rhodes interview is thirty minutes long, and each finalist gets a scheduled slot chosen at random. The interviews start midmorning and go straight through the afternoon. The finalists had drawn numbers at the reception the night before to determine time slots. I drew one thirty in the afternoon, but the time didn't really matter to me. I got to the library early so I could be totally relaxed when I went in to the face the committee members.

The questions the Rhodes judges ask are tailored to the candidate. Some can seem like very strange things to ask, but the judges want to see more than just a display of knowledge; they want to see how a person thinks in an extemporaneous fashion. They are looking for genuine answers with authentic feelings and thoughtfulness behind them. They are measuring your answers for much more than just the content, for something beyond the words you use.

The first question after I sat down in front of all the judges at their long wooden table in the hushed and somber rare books reading room was, "Given the economic structure of the NCAA and the various and competing stakeholders, what kind of model could serve to pay NCAA athletes without completely disrupting the system of college athletics?" For a second it seemed like a daunting and complex question. Sure, sports talk show hosts regularly debate the idea of paying student athletes because a lot of scholarships leave students hungry, with no extra money even for some essentials. Or, furthermore, college coaches make millions off the labor of their athletes who are not allowed to receive financial compensation above tuition, room, board, and stipend. But this was a deeper question than that. And I knew the committee was looking for a deeper answer than the usual talk-show sound bites.

To be honest, I wasn't quite sure what my answer would be. I said, "Let me think for a second." I looked out the window as I thought, and I could see the top of the Union Bank building where I worked in high school. Then the answer came to me, all at once.

"In high school, I worked at Union Bank. You can see the building right out that window. I was mentored by the president of the Union Bank Foundation, the nonprofit arm that was established after the Community Reinvestment Act was voted into law in 1977. In addition to ending redlining and other racist bank practices, the act required that the bank invest a percentage of their profits back into the community the bank served. Wouldn't it be amazing if Division I colleges used that same model to reward student athletes? A small percentage of things like TV revenue or ticket sales could go toward ensuring athletes will transition to successful careers and lives after their athletic careers are over. Like some type of pension, similar to that of the professional leagues."

Then they asked me, "What does it mean to be a Rhodes Scholar?"

Without hesitating, I recited Tupac's poem "The Rose That Grew from Concrete." I said, "That's me, that rose. If you were all walking together and you saw a rose growing up out of a crack in the concrete, a place where there's no soil, limited sunlight, no water . . . you would all marvel at that sight." I looked at the judge who had asked the question. "That's what you see when you look at me. You see a rose that grew from the concrete. A rose that made it all the way here. The Rhodes Scholarship embodies all the impossible dreams that got me here and my own fierce struggle out of systemic inner-city poverty that is structured to limit your hopes, dreams, and expectations of self."

The interview went on like that, with a series of topics

that hit home with me. Though the questions were academic in nature, I related every single thing they asked to something I had learned in my life. It would have been easy enough to answer with a multiplicity of readings, theories, and philosophical responses, but I wanted to speak from my core. I was able to respond candidly and forcefully. I answered each question with as much authenticity as I could. I talked about everything in my past, about my mother and her fight to raise us, about my father and the shame of knowing he was behind bars for murder. I talked about my community and the strategies and methodologies I'd use to improve it. The time flew by and almost before I knew it, I was sitting out in the hall with all the other finalists as we waited for the committee to decide on the two winners.

Everybody was stupid nervous. When people are nervous, what they do is talk a lot. So all these Ivy League kids were talking about what they accomplished in their interviews. It was mostly, "What was your pitch?" and "This was my pitch." It kind of annoyed me, the way they were trying to measure each other's worth. I just sat there quietly, sitting on a library bench, minding my business. We waited for what seemed like a long time. Eventually I put in my earphones and watched some dance videos on my phone. I think these other kids might have thought it was strange that I wasn't saying anything, that I was comfortable just sitting there keeping to myself. But I had done all my talking. I had made my case. Nicole and another young woman from MIT had gotten curious a few times and included me in the conversation, but for the most part the larger group didn't pay me much mind. They didn't see me as an intellectual threat, so they gravitated to the more loquacious people who might have what they in their minds considered a legitimate chance at winning. Now was the time for silent reflection and waiting. Waiting doesn't always need to be noisy. I can lean into discomfort. I can be very comfortable in silence.

The light in the tall windows of the library began to fade to dusk. The other kids wore themselves out and fell quiet, leaning against walls or slumped in chairs. Some of them kept checking their watches. Finally, at six thirty they called us into the reading room. The judges were all standing there looking very serious. Judge Karen Stevenson stood in front of the other committee members and looked at the finalists, moving her gaze from face to face. "We've had a great selection of finalists this year. I'm very proud of how far all of you have come. I don't want to make this too grandiose or let the tension build too much. So we're going to go ahead and announce the Rhodes Scholars. Immediately afterward, I'd like those two people to come with me because we have some business we have to handle upstairs."

Everyone was fidgeting. I braced myself, in case I lost. I thought, *Let me get myself ready*, but then I stopped myself and thought, *Nah, scrap all that. I won. Caylin Moore is a Rhodes Scholar.* I repeated that thought in my head as Judge Stevenson said, "The first 2017 Rhodes Scholar from District 16 is . . . Nicole Mihelson." Nicole smiled as people next to her gave her nervous congratulatory nods and smiles. They were okay with her winning, because nobody in the room felt that he or she had lost. Yet.

Judge Stevenson continued, "And without further ado, our second winner for the 2017 Rhodes Scholarship is Caylin Louis Moore." There it was. As it turned out, I was literally the last 2017 Rhodes Scholar chosen, out of all the thirty-two across the country. It was only right. Last, but definitely not least.

There was silence as the selections sank in and the rest of the young men and women in that room processed the fact that they hadn't won. The already dense quiet of the Los Angeles Public Library wrapped around us and seemed even heavier than normal. Nobody moved. I leaned my head forward so that my dreads would form a drape to hide my face, because I was crying. I was crying tears of joy, and I was crying tears of sorrow for the others like me still stuck in the hood, and for all the things I had gone through to be in that place at that moment. I stood there posted in my best "young bull" pose—eyes down, feet apart, shoulders square, standing tall. I was solid and unshakable. "Ten toes down" is what they call it where I'm from. But I wasn't posing. I was purely overwhelmed.

As the tears filled my eyes, I stared down at the only pair of dress shoes I owned and kept my hands folded in front of me.

I had to take those long, stretched-out seconds to process the reality of what had just happened. It was almost like some sort of weird justice for a father doing life in prison for murder, and a mother who was raped in the hospital as she recovered from open-heart surgery. I felt like I was living proof of God's unmerited favor and the fact that with pure hard work and faith, we can come back, make it through anything, and rise to win. That moment validated all those hours spent digging through recycling bins for sticky returnable Miller bottles and Coke cans. My youth football fees, one nickel at a time. All those times we had run out of money at the end of the month and there was simply no food in the house. Bucket baths and four to a bed. All of it.

My mind flashed back to the late-night gunfire and police helicopters that would regularly wake me up as a kid. I thought about the rats and roaches always making little scratching noises inside the walls of our sad, beat-up house.

Grow up in Compton and any dreams that take you beyond that place are dreams too big. It's not realistic to imagine yourself in a room with—much less in competition with—students from Harvard, Yale, MIT, and UCLA. But beat them? To be measured and tested by a group of former Rhodes Scholars—judges, doctors, politicians—and find that you come out on top? That's simply inconceivable. Yet here I was, with my place in that room, my feet as firm to the ground as a metal pole in dried cement. All I could think was, *Thank God, thank Jesus. You are amazing, Lord. I give all thanks, praise, and honor to you. Thank you.*

I realized that I had been frozen in place for half a minute and the rest of the group was waiting. I had hesitated because stepping forward represented my silent acceptance that anything was possible. For about thirty-seven seconds I wasn't ready to accept that. This moment was my entrance into a limitless new world, and stepping into it had to be done thoughtfully so that I didn't forget the lessons behind me. I waited a few seconds more, lifted my head, stepped forward, and took Judge Stevenson's outstretched hand firmly in mine, accepting her congratulations. Everyone applauded politely, but I felt like shouting to the heavens. This wasn't an occasion to be quiet.

I called my mom before doing anything else. I could feel my voice trembling, and I could barely hold back the tears.

"Mom, I'm a Rhodes Scholar."

I could hear the knot form in her throat and the tears well up in her eyes. She said, "Baby, I gotta go."

I understood. She needed to go spend some time on

hands and knees thanking God and praising. That was fine with me. My mom had poured all the love and wisdom she could into me. This was validation of her faith in God's goodness and of her own effort to help me realize all my potential. She had worked so hard. She had struggled through counseling in the years after her sexual assault and the crippling anxiety she had experienced from that evil act. She had gone on to give back to the community and the church, providing church members with low-cost legal services. Eventually she had gone on to coach at Los Angeles Southwest College. She mentored many young men at the college, kids who had seen all kinds of things—they had been shot at, abused by their parents, and worse. Some had criminal records or drug problems. She tried her best to light a way forward for each and every one of them, but she couldn't be sure whether they would make it to where they needed to go. She must have experienced so much disappointment in the knowledge that she couldn't save all the starfish on the beach. But here, for a moment, she realized how far I had come with her help. As much as for other reasons, I had worked for the Rhodes Scholarship to honor her.

Like running downhill, things sped up from that moment. Judge Stevenson took Nicole and me upstairs, where we filled out a package of paperwork while she called Washington, DC, to let the president of the American Rhodes Trust know that the final selections for the 2017 Rhodes Scholarship had been made. Once we were done with the paperwork, I called my sister and brother and let them know I had won. I texted the TCU press office to let them know I had won, because they wanted to put out a press release as soon as the decision was made. Then I called Paola. She picked up the phone on the third ring, and I could tell that she had run to get it.

"Paola, *mi amor*. I'm a Rhodes Scholar!"

8

QUESTION: *"How will you contribute to the legacy of Rhodes Scholars?"*

I like to live low-key, with as much quiet and solitude as possible. But in my last months at TCU, I didn't get much chance; my phone blew up with requests for interviews and appearances. It seemed like everyone wanted a piece of me, and I still needed to get ready to move to England. I had gotten so much local press and on-campus coverage that I couldn't even go to the dining hall or computer lab without other students stopping me to ask questions and congratulate me on winning the Rhodes. It seemed like everybody in the whole world knew. All that attention only got more intense after Lester Holt did a special on me for *NBC Nightly News*. It wasn't a documentary, but it took almost as much of my time between doing the actual interview sessions, getting mic'd up, being prepped to go on camera, and answering all the follow-up questions the producers kept hitting me with.

I was busier than I had ever been. I wanted to spend as much time as possible balancing my normal life in and out of the classroom, but I also wanted to take advantage of all the press opportunities to show other young black men it was possible to have big dreams come true. And, as ever, I stayed in close contact with my family.

Mi was working as a nurse and had made a nice life for herself and my beautiful newborn niece, Delanie. Chase had realized a dream he had from when he was eight years old. His dreams began one night when we were having a rare meal out at Sizzler, and Chase saw the USC Trojans play the University of Texas Longhorns on a TV in a corner of the restaurant. Chase was amazed that the team with the "cows on their helmets" beat the California powerhouse USC. He decided right then and there that he wanted to go to the University of Texas and play for the Longhorns. Even though he was practically illiterate at the time—a result of his poor education at our elementary school—he set himself the goal of going to the University of Texas, at a time when he couldn't spell *university* or even *Texas*. He never lost that dream, and after a year and a half at Holy Cross he had transferred to UT, earning a place on the football team. He even started a SPARK chapter on campus. He kept as busy as I did.

The upside to being so busy was that time moved fast. Graduation was on me before I knew it. It was satisfying to know I was moving to the next goal. But as I had with Verbum Dei, I didn't see graduating TCU as a life-changing experience. Getting a college degree had always been an expectation. From the time I was six or seven, my mom had made it clear that it was not a matter of *if* I was going to college but rather which college I would be graduating from. Most of my teachers at Dodson and all my teachers at Verbum Dei assumed every student was meant to go on to college. They gave you the tools, and you were supposed to use them to your best advantage. That mind-set had been drilled into me, and I had come to believe that it should be drilled into all kids in my community. Many of the most intractable problems plaguing impoverished inner-city neighborhoods across the country can be traced to substandard public schools and the resulting lack of educational expectations, as well as a misunderstanding of the opportunities education presents. All those problems can be traced back to slavery. The bar for educational standards in Compton and places like it should be set every bit as high, if not higher, than it is in more affluent neighborhoods.

The best part of graduation was getting to spend some time with the people who meant the most to me. Paola was in the final rounds of the hammer throw for the Big 12 Conference championships, so she was out of town, but my mom, my sister, one of my aunties, a couple of my cousins, and even Coach Johnson from the Falcons were in the audience to see me walk. A graduation is never short on emotion. So, to capitalize on the moment, I gave everyone a little show to lighten things up when I was called up to get my diploma. After I shook Chancellor Boschini's hand and stopped to take a picture with him, I hit a light Milly Rock dance as I walked across the stage. It was only right.

A week after graduation, Paola and I took off to her native Paraguay for her South American Games track-and-field competition. I had never been to South America, and the trip was an amazing education. It gave me the chance to see where Paola had grown up, to learn more about her homeland and culture, and—more importantly—to meet her family. Driving from the airport to her home over roads of large rocks and cement, I came to understand why my girlfriend has such a humble spirit and positive outlook. Her parents live in a modest house in a quiet, family-oriented neighborhood of Lambaré, the sixth-largest city in the country. Lambaré borders the capital of Asunción and has busy markets and many food vendors. The third night we were there, Paola's family threw a cookout party. Paraguayans are masters of cooking on the grill, and the meal was course after course of delicious meats—rich grilled steaks, grilled sausages with cheese in the center, and tender pork ribs. There were grilled vegetables as well, including charred mandioca, the starchy root so common in Latin America. We drank the traditional beverage called *cocido*, a tea of boiled yerba mate. We snacked on the indigenous cheese bread known as *chipa* and finished with a light dessert of tropical fruits like guava and Brazilian mangoes.

The night was just warm enough, a beautiful evening full of family and fun. Finally, after the meal, I danced slowly with Paola on the patio to "Love" by Musiq Soulchild. It couldn't have been a better choice, because at the end of the song, I let go of her, backed up a step, and—with her family watching—got down on one knee. I read her a poem I had written, speaking in Spanish. Although I come from Afro-Latino roots on my mother's side, and I'm from a majority Spanish-speaking area of Los Angeles, I didn't grow up speaking Spanish. I started studying Spanish late at night beginning in February of my last year at TCU, in preparation for this moment. It was important for me to propose to her in her native tongue. "*Te amo*" means a lot more to her than "I love you."

> My little bear, my beautiful,
> I love you, Paola, I love you.
> I love your siblings, your mother, your father.
> I love the ground you walk on.
> I appreciate how you accept me as I am,
> flaws and everything.
> You don't see me as a poor kid,
> who grew up in Compton,
> with only my mom and my siblings,
> and the rats and cockroaches in the walls.
> You see me how the Lord sees me,
> as a king who will one day change the world.
> I now know why God had me come to TCU.
> I now know why I went through everything that
>   I did.
> I know why I went to the bank that day,

and met you walking on campus.
Because every king needs a queen.
I will grow old with you,
and one day die a happy man, a grateful man,
when I go on to meet the Father.
Paola, will you marry me?

I had hidden the ring in my sock, just like the many kids who have to put their wallets and phones in their socks when they ride the city bus, so that the gang members find nothing when they pat them down for a "pocket check." I pulled the ring out and held it up to her. Thank goodness, after all that, she said, "Yes."

It was fortunate that I bought the ring at a store that had a return policy. After a week back home in Fort Worth, I could tell that Paola had something she wanted to talk to me about but was reluctant to bring up.

"What's wrong, *mi amor*? Are you okay?"

She smiled, "Sí. But the ring . . ."

"You don't like it?"

"I don't really like the history behind diamonds. How many people have died because of these stupid stones? I don't like it when women say, 'Oh, you're engaged, let me see your hand.' It feels so materialistic that people get so excited about a ring. This girl even told me at work, 'I would definitely marry any guy if he gave me a ring like that.'"

I totally understood. The religious and cultural beliefs Paola and I share give us a similar view of marriage. It has nothing to do with rings or material goods. It's like an isosceles triangle with God at the top point, and Paola and me at the two bottom points. The closer both of us get to God, the closer we get to each other and the better things will work out for our relationship. The further we are from God, the further we will be from one another. We're not naive; we understand that two people don't always have the same perspective on everything in life. That's a good thing; it helps iron sharpen iron. But you need to share core values. Paola and I both value humility in the face of God and supporting each other in our spirituality. Those values are so strong that they hold us together and give us the tools to navigate the rest of life.

We returned the ring when we got back to California. We drove our rental car to Carson Mall. We bought a simple gold band instead. Then we put the rest of the money in a college fund for the children we planned to have.

We were married two months later on August 15. We took our vows in a small chapel in Norwalk, a pretty little city about sixteen miles southeast of downtown Los Angeles. We had a small, intimate wedding, with six guests and no frills. Paola wore a modern, beautiful white dress and I wore a suit. We walked the sand at Hermosa

Beach right afterward. Barefoot on warm sand, excited about our new life together.

We spent our honeymoon in Oxford. Although Paola had been to Spain, France, and other places in Europe for international track-and-field competitions, she had never been to England. We had decided to spend our honeymoon there so that both of us could check out where I would be living, and for me to get a better sense of the city before I hit the ground running in graduate school. I also wanted to show her how beautiful that part of England is. We stayed at the elegant Macdonald Randolph Hotel, a fixture in central Oxford. It's a five-star hotel that was built in 1864, but with a Gothic style that makes it fit right in with the much older buildings in Oxford. The hotel was incredibly luxurious; every detail was beautiful and elegant. There were little adjustable reading lights on flexible arms that stuck out from each side of the headboard, and the sheets were the softest I'd ever felt. It was more luxurious than any place I had ever stayed. The hotel was perfectly located, close to everything we wanted to see. Mostly we spent the week just walking around the city, taking in the sights, and talking about how far we had come.

When we got back to Texas, I got busy preparing for the next big step in my life. I spoke at a few universities around the nation, went to visit my brother down at the University of Texas, and took care of a lot of other little details to prepare for moving to England. Most difficult of all, I kissed my wife goodbye. She was in her final year at TCU. Not even thousands of miles and two month-long semesters could break our bond. We both had some business to take care of and knew that God would permanently bring us back together under one roof as soon as possible. Finally, in the last week of September, I boarded a flight from Dallas-Fort Worth to Washington, DC. The Rhodes committee sponsors a weekend in the nation's capital they call the Rhodes Bon Voyage weekend. It's where all thirty-two of the American Rhodes Scholars for that year gather and get to know one another. There is an orientation session for new Scholars, and there are a lot of opportunities to meet previous Rhodes Scholars to ask them questions and get perspectives. The centerpiece of the weekend is a reception and keynote speech, followed the next day by a departure luncheon before everyone flies out.

That weekend gave me a chance to process this adventure I was about to undertake. Spending time with all the other Rhodes Scholars, seeing that they were just as excited as I was, made me realize I was part of something bigger than myself. I wasn't on this journey alone. We were all a part of a long tradition of academics, part of a long line of people seeking to change the world in their own individual way. I realized that as much as it was an opportunity, the Rhodes was also an obligation. Not just to myself but to my community—an obligation to ultimately bring back wisdom and tools for liberation. That sense of responsibility made me hungrier than ever to get after it. I was really excited to get started on my Oxford education.

The flight to London's Heathrow Airport was the first of many joint activities all the scholars would share before we headed off to our education and our different paths through life. I had a lot of luggage because I didn't know what it would be like living in Oxford year-round. I felt like I should prepare for any situation. I brought hiking boots, cold-weather gear, warm-weather clothes, and all kinds of stuff. I even packed five suits and dress shoes because I thought many events at Oxford would be formal. The program had booked all thirty-two of us in one section of the plane.

As everyone was getting settled in their seats, I slipped on my headphones but I didn't put on any music, and I closed my eyes to get a little rest. But I could still hear what was being said around me. It was a way to learn more about my fellow Scholars—to understand their perspectives—without just speaking about myself. I heard people analyze politics, gender dynamics, and broad issues of diversity. They went over a range of perspectives on many different topics that I had never had the opportunity to hear before. It made me excited to talk with everyone individually in Oxford.

It's a little more than a seven-hour flight from Washington, DC, to London. We got in a little bit tired, but we were all eager to get to Oxford and settle in. The Rhodes House porter, Bob Wyllie, met us outside the baggage claim and led us to a huge, comfortable bus. Bob is a Rhodes legend, beloved by Rhodes Scholars for his welcoming nature, his down-to-earth sense of humor, and his overall helpfulness. He is a slightly rumpled, white-haired grandpa type, and he's usually found next to his lovely wife, Dawn. They seem to enjoy the world immensely, and laughter is the soundtrack of their lives.

It took an hour to get to Oxford by bus. The best part of the trip was seeing Oxford from a totally different viewpoint from when I had been there as a tourist on my honeymoon. The city slowly unfolded as the bus went from college to college, dropping off Scholars at each one.

The University of Oxford isn't just one place or one campus. It takes up most of the city and is composed of thirty-eight distinct and autonomous colleges, and six Permanent Private Halls (though similar to the colleges, these were founded by individual Christian denominations and are smaller in size). Driving slowly throughout Oxford, you discover that each college has its own identity as well. The different locations are like the neighborhoods, each with its own individual character. I had requested St. John's College as my first choice, with Magdalen and Merton Colleges as my backups. I chose them because they were three of the largest colleges in Oxford and I figured they probably had the best assets, like bigger libraries, better computer labs, or bigger travel-abroad grants. But the truth is, every college at Oxford is incredibly well equipped. And in my life, divine intervention pops up all the time. I didn't get my first three choices because those colleges did not have tutors in my chosen focus of Latin American Studies. The college that did? Jesus College. When I found out which college I was assigned to, I thought, *Oh yeah, we know who set that up.*

Jesus College dates from 1571 and was established through a royal charter decreed by Queen Elizabeth I. Like all the colleges at Oxford, Jesus College has a long and incredible history and has produced remarkable leaders and thinkers since its founding. I was happy to land there, and felt like it was part of a divine plan.

In any case, Oxford was going to be comfortable for me. On campus, students at Jesus College are assigned their own studio apartments with a sink and a shared bathroom. Mine was spacious and comfortable, with a big bed and plenty of room to spread out—the biggest room I had ever lived in up to that point. It overlooked Cornmarket Street, which is the busiest road in Oxford. Shoppers mix with street vendors and performers like jugglers to make Cornmarket a vibrant place day or night. I loved the location. The apartment gave me quick access to the dining hall, and it was close to Jesus College's library, where I was going to be spending a lot of time. I especially loved going to the dining hall at Jesus College, which truly looked like something out of a Harry Potter movie. I was always warmly greeted by Bruno Mollier, a Frenchman who is in charge of the dining services, as well as the many support staff members from Spain who provided me a daily opportunity to work on my Spanish.

Although each college has its own identity, they all follow the Oxford method of study and offer a full range of degree topics. Rhodes Scholars can choose their area of study and can get two master's degrees in two one-year programs, or a two-year master's of philosophy, or a earn a doctorate of philosophy over a three-year course. I decided to pursue a master's in Latin American Studies in my first year and to use that time to decide what to study the subsequent year or if I wanted to begin doctoral work elsewhere.

Regardless of the program focus, the methodology Oxford colleges use is the same. Unlike most American universities, a course at Oxford involves attending classes and writing essays that are not turned in to be graded. Instead, a tutorial system is used. The student sits down with a tutor or the professor and together they go over the essay to critically analyze it. Other students are welcome to participate. It's a deeply cerebral approach to learning, and it requires a lot of critical thought.

This process makes you approach essay writing and topical thinking in a totally different way. For example, for one tutorial I wrote an essay on the Cuban Revolution.

In most college classes it would be easy to be somewhat dry or even a little flippant, just trying to fulfill the assignment and make a grade. But when you realize that a Cuban student will be reviewing the essay and giving you oral criticism, the exercise takes on a much more immediate intensity. As a result, you become more adept at articulating your thinking and making an argument. Getting these kinds of multiple perspectives on any topic you attack is a key part of an Oxford education. The process continues through the school year, culminating in a dissertation. And to be awarded a degree, you have to take final exams, which are not administered by your specific college but by the university. The rigorous nature of the process really appealed to me. There were so many opportunities for deep learning, not only from books and research but from professors and other students as well.

But for me, this wasn't education for education's sake.

I never, ever lose sight of where I come from. Everything I do relates to who I was, who I am, and who I hope to become. But it has zero to do with what's "best" for me. It's about whom, other than God, I will serve. I'm not focusing on Latin American Studies because that's my sole burning passion. I chose that topic because I'm married to a Latin American woman, and this degree will make me a more understanding companion. I also come from Latin American roots on my mother's side; studying this course will help me understand myself. And I chose it to gain a better contextual history of Latin America, to expand my understanding of the world at large and the struggles of all indigenous peoples and African-descended peoples. Whether I ultimately go into academia, law, or politics, a background in Latin American studies will strengthen my writing and research skills, and will broaden my perspective in my fight to help others.

I look at Los Angeles and I see many of the problems and challenges I dealt with in my youth still persisting. I want to be a force that propels that change, for my community and all the communities like it. I know how that change happens—one person, one young man or woman, at a time.

There is so much confusion on all sides of the issues of poverty and race in this country. They are maybe the biggest challenges America faces. My own mother was born at a time when blacks were regularly denied the right to vote through poll taxes, violent terrorism, and other unconstitutional tactics. My grandparents both left the South to get away from the ugliness of racism in Tennessee and Texas, only to be confronted by more subtle forms of racism in California. They left a place where "separate but equal" was a new normal, to enter a place where discriminatory housing and banking practices became the new normal.

Growing up in Compton, I realize that we may not be as far away from the Civil Rights Act of 1964 as many would like to assume. This act brought forth integration in public places, but somehow forgot to bring integration in land ownership, business ownership, and political power. Where I'm from, we never saw the Ku Klux Klan or pickup trucks with the Confederate flag. But we saw the rise of the prison-industrial complex. I didn't know of any lynchings in the hood, like what was done to Emmett Till as a punishment for whistling at a white woman. But I grew up witnessing the results of mandatory minimum sentencing, the "three strikes" law, and the crack epidemic in Los Angeles. It confused me as a kid that the judicial system came to the hood to find drugs and drug abusers, when I'm sure they could have easily found tons of both at the music festivals, such as Coachella and Stagecoach that my white friends from middle school went to. These are not systems that were created by people in du-rags and hoodies; they were instituted by people in suits and cufflinks.

Even if we look at things such as gang violence, drug crime, and theft, they all have their roots in the long period of systemic deprivation in the United States. Over that time, there has always been a strong pushback against efforts to change the tide of the status quo. The pushback was strong enough for some people to murder two presidents, the most prominent civil rights figure in history, and a fourteen-year-old little black boy.

Despite our history, I am still encouraged by how the

status quo is changing, and I am inspired by the indomitable spirit of a downtrodden group of people. As my mom always said, "Like cream in coffee, we will still rise to the top." I am also inspired by those of different backgrounds who choose to be the champions of causes in my community and for all people. I'm also hopeful for the future, given the changes we have seen in this nation, and I'm excited to see how things will improve during my lifetime. But my experience alone serves as a testament to the fact that we still have work to do.

These are the simple facts of our history. We must not be made uncomfortable by discussions of race and poverty in this country, lest we become complicit in their persistence. Instead of thinking only about all the recent instances of police brutality or black-on-black violence, we must collectively, as brothers and sisters of all backgrounds, take a deep, hard look at the history. We must come to grips with the fact that there has never been a time period in this nation when "all lives mattered," and there especially hasn't been a time period when black lives mattered.

I no longer fear a gun held by a black hand, nor do I fear a gun held by a police officer. Now I fear a black hand without a book in it more than I fear anything else in my community. I don't know what the answer is, nor do I believe that there is a simple solution. But I do know that you have to constantly fight to change perspectives. You have to expose youth to the possibilities in the world and then encourage them along any path toward those possibilities. But most importantly, we must create systems that make it feasible for the youth to actually manifest those possibilities.

Thankfully I've had many opportunities of exposure and encouragement. My next dream, a dream that might be too big, is to reach every single child in the world with the same kind of exposure and encouragement that I received. I might not be able to help every child, but I pray that I will inspire one child who touches others. That's why I'm so focused on having an impact directly on the youth. I can't go a single day without speaking life into a dying situation with the youth I mentor, speaking through a microphone or encountering them in the streets. I had a mentor tell me, "There is only one way to find yourself. You must lose yourself in the service of others." I feel a strong responsibility to serve in my heart. In one way or another, I will continue to do this for the rest of my life.

That kind of responsibility, the drive to have a positive impact, is part of what I will pass on to my children. My first child, a beautiful little girl, was born on July 23, 2018. I always call my wife *mi amor*, which is Spanish for "my love." Love is the foundation of our relationship. On our wedding day, when the pastor asked my wife if she would take me to be her lawfully wedded husband, she misheard and said, "I take Caylin Moore to be my lovely husband." Considering that my last name is Moore, it is only fitting that we named our little girl Mia. Mia Moore. Our daughter will have no middle name, because we believe that nothing should get in between love. Paola and I hope to raise more children in the future. They will be part of my new legacy, and I hope they will also be part of the legacy of change for places like Compton and, ultimately, the world at large.

Children are an incredible blessing, the highest expression of what we as humans can do—create a life. Parenting is a spiritual connection, a very special gift God gives us. We get to enjoy wisdom, guidance, and love because we are all children of the Most High. Those are the least a parent can give their own children. Paola and I consider the children we have as divine gifts. They won't be our children—they will be God's children, and we'll raise them with the same care and devotion we give to the Lord. I will pour into my children the knowledge, self-respect, dignity, and faith that my mother poured into me.

But I also see them as vessels, carrying a vision for a better world. I think, *Wow, what a powerful thing that would be, what an incredible legacy to have, if I could bring more lights into a dark world.* Not only will we change the world by the things we do, we'll also hope to raise individuals from the beginning to change the world. We'll love them and encourage them from as early an age as possible. Man, that is a powerful thing. That is perhaps the most meaningful thing I can do—be a great father.

My mom is about as excited at the prospect of grandkids as we are about having children. She has made it to a place of comfort in her life. After all she went through, all the suffering and trials, she is settled within herself. As nervous as she was about me playing tackle football, it's ironic that she became the director of football operations for the athletics department at Los Angeles Southwest College, and is now a college football coach in training. Even if my mom never becomes a Nick Saban-caliber head coach, I know that she will use this opportunity to engage with young men of color as her ministry, to help them use the sport as a stepping stone to their own dreams.

Stepping stones built on a strong foundation are imperative if you are going to build anything of substance. My mom, the Snoop League, Verbum Dei, Marist, Bristol, Princeton, TCU, and now Oxford have been stepping stones in my evolution. Those people and places gave me the strength and opportunities to grow, to learn, and to become a better man. Even with all of the work and effort, it still almost didn't happen. With the help of God and my family, I came to realize that there is no such thing as a dream too big. Yeah, you might fight to realize your biggest dreams and still fall short. But that, too, is part of growing and getting better. At the end of the day, in shooting for those big goals, those things that seem impossible and unattainable, your hard work and dedication will be put to their best use. No matter what happens, something great will come of everything you put into chasing those big dreams. As my story shows, you may find that on your way to a dream too big to come true, you are rewarded with something even bigger and better.

Acknowledgments

Writing this book has been an incredible journey. The challenges of creating something out of nothing are indescribable. I am eternally grateful to the many people who played a part in getting this project into motion. I am also thankful for the consortium of people that I have drawn strength and inspiration from for this particular work.

To my family, I want to thank all of you for your continued support throughout this life journey. Seen and unseen. Thank you to my incredible wife, Paola Moore, my daughter, Mia Moore, and all my future descendants.

This book is a paean to my mother. Mom, the English language doesn't have the sufficient vocabulary for me to describe how grateful I am. Mom, know that I was listening and paying attention the whole time. Mom, I love you. Dad, I love you. Thank you.

To my ancestors, both immediate and distant, thank you for the sacrifices that you made for me to be here today. Thank you to my ancestors who passed away in those middle passage slave ships, to those that chose death in the Atlantic Ocean over bondage in the land of the free, to those that miraculously survived the middle passage, to those that endured hundreds of years of bondage, to those that rebelled, to the thousands of strange fruits that hung by the neck from trees in the United States between the Civil War and World War II. To those that fought in the American Revolution and in every single American War. Thank you. It is because of your mortal sacrifices that I am here today. In your memory, I live. Let this never be forgotten, lest it be repeated. May I carry myself in a way that dignifies and honors you. Ancestors, may your spirit and faith be with me that I may never be discouraged in my fight for humanity.

I extend my deepest gratitude to those that paved the way for me to be here. Thank you to my heroes Marian Wright Edelman, Ella Baker, Sojourner Truth, Angela Y. Davis, Calynn J. Taylor Moore, Michelle Obama, Marielle Franco, Rosa Parks, Ida B. Wells, Ava DuVernay, Harriet Tubman, Nat Turner, Telemaque, Vicente Ramón Guerrero Saldaña, Jean-Jacques Dessalines, Fred Hampton, Sengbe Pieh, Toussaint Louverture, Spike Lee, Marcus Garvey, Nelson Mandela, and Malcolm X.

Thank you to my athletic heroes and inspirations, Venus Williams, Serena Williams, Wilma Rudolph, John Carlos, Tommie Smith, Pelé, Colin Kaepernick, Arthur

Ashe, Myron Rolle, Muhammad Ali, Andre Ward, Stafon Johnson, LeBron James, Damian Lillard, and Wayne Simpson.

Lauryn Hill, Wale, Meek Mill, Immortal Technique, Blu and Exile, J. Cole, Tupac, and Kendrick Lamar: thank you for giving me music to listen to and connect with during those lonely nights with only a deck of cards and a hard garage floor to do pushups.

Thank you to my greatest writing inspirations: Maya Angelou, Michelle Alexander, Toni Morrison, Chimamanda Ngozi Adichi, Angela J. Davis, Black Ice, Michael Eric Dyson, Cornel West, James Baldwin, Father Greg Boyle, Ta-Nahesi Coates, Wes Moore, Paolo Freire, Alex Haley, and Bryan Stevenson.

Thank you to my many mentors that taught me that one must have boots in order to pull themselves up from their bootstraps.

Thank you to everyone from my village. Thank you to Ms. Blanchard, for yelling at me every time I rode my bicycle on your grass; that's where I learned the concept of boundaries. Thank you to the mailman who showed up on time every single day; that's where I learned punctuality. Thank you to "New Neighbor," who was always cleaning up around the house and yard; that's where I learned the importance of organization. Thank you to Coach Wadood, from the Snoop League; it is through your example that I learned the importance of being a man of my community. Thank you to Wayne Simpson, MLB pitcher, for telling me that I had a good arm.

Special thanks to Jane Dystel for encouraging me to write this book and connecting all the dots for me to make this a reality.

Extreme gratitude to Chris Peterson for your many contributions to this project. From questioning word choice, to helping me think critically about communicating my story, I am grateful for all of it. I'm thankful to have had a fresh eye on the book, guidance on timelines and encouragement for the process whenever it was needed.

The entire Thomas Nelson team deserves tremendous credit. Thank you for venturing out into deeper waters and embracing a conversation that has been long overdue. Webster Younce, my editor, helped me bring out granular details of my life and showed me why they are important—thank you for pushing me. Thank you to Brigitta Nortker, for your readings of the manuscript and your keen eye for details. Thank you to Karin Silver, my copyeditor, for all of your innumerable contributions. Thank you to Karen Jackson and Sara Broun for all your efforts in promoting and marketing the book.

Love, honor, and praise to the Most High.

About the Author

CAYLIN LOUIS MOORE grew up in Compton, California. A graduate of Texas Christian University, he went on to become a 2017 Rhodes Scholar. His graduate studies were performed at the University of Oxford, Jesus College. Moore and his wife, Paola, have one daughter, Mia.